SAPIENTIA ET DOCTRINA STABILITAS

Still Running...

Personal stories by Queen's women
celebrating the fiftieth anniversary
of the Marty Scholarship

Edited by
JOY PARR

Foreword by
PAULINE JEWETT, MP

Queen's University Alumnae Association

© Queen's University Alumnae Association, 1987

Graphic Design: Peter Dorn, RCA, FGDC

Canadian Cataloguing in Publication Data
Main entry under title:

Still running –

ISBN 0-88911-507-9

1. Queen's University (Kingston, Ont.) – Biography.
2. Women college graduates – Canada – Biography.
3. Women – Canada – Biography. 4. Marty Memorial Scholarship. I. Parr, Joy, 1949–
II. Queen's University (Kingston, Ont.). Alumnae Association.

FC25.S75 1987   920.72'0971   C87-094676-5
F1005.S75 1987

The painting reproduced on the cover is by Lee Kozlik, Marty Scholar for 1985, who donated it to the Queen's Alumnae Collection. Titled, *Ultraschall/Ultrasound*, it is oil on canvas, 210cm by 375 cm.

Still Running...

Contents

Part Two
1959-1987

Pauline Jewett, Simon Fraser University, September 1974. Welcoming rally for the new President. CREDIT: Ed Chan, SFU/IMC.

Foreword

As a Marty holder myself I am honoured to be asked to write a brief foreword to this volume of essays by other Marty scholars.

It's a grand book. I only wish Jean Royce were alive to read it: she who did so much for so many of us. If it hadn't been for Jean cajoling me into applying for the Marty in 1949 to do post-doctoral studies I would never have finished my PhD thesis. I could hardly have embarked on post-doctoral studies without a doctorate!

I love the breadth and sweep of the book, the diversity of approach ranging from Joyce Hemlow's marvellously documented unveiling of the Fanny Burney manuscripts and papers to Priscilla Galloway's moving account of her struggle for intellectual survival. While diverse in approach there is, nevertheless, a common theme throughout. That theme is the seemingly ever present hurdles – then and now – to the realization of the full potential of individual women and women everywhere.

Reading these essays is an experience that is both heartening and heartwarming, if sometimes chilling too. Wit, style and intellect abound. May I, on behalf of all Marty scholars, thank our sisters, the contributors, for having done us proud.

Pauline Jewett, MP

Introduction

JOY PARR

We began this book several years ago as a way to mark the fiftieth anniversary of a remarkable scholarship – the Marty Memorial – established, funded and administered by women graduates of Queen's University in Kingston, Ontario, to help women students pursue advanced work. We began modestly, hoping only to locate the Marty Scholars and compile enough information to write brief biographical notes about each. As the months passed our conception of the project began to change. The replies to our inquiries were full of laughter, warmth and wry wisdom. The more we learned about these women and their careers in the arts, letters, science, industry and public service, the more we wanted to know. About this time Margaret Gillett and Kay Sibbald published a collection of autobiographies by McGill women, called *A Fair Shake*.[1] As our copies of their book grew comfortably worn, we were encouraged to approach the Marty Scholars again, this time asking for their own autobiographical reflections on their lives as scholars, teachers and as women.

Writing about one's self is not easy, and may be especially difficult for women, unaccustomed as we are to seeing ourselves as subjects. It is, in any case, like planting annuals and fishing for trout, a task to be undertaken only in due season. Brazenly and unilaterally, we declared the summer of 1986 the season of retrospection for Marty Scholars. Sensibly, some wrote back to tell us that our appointed time was not theirs. Some we never reached. But for others the moment did seem right and some, who in correspondence described their lives as uneventful or unworthy, enclosed essays filled with adventure, achievement, compassion and insight. Shortened versions of fifteen of the replies appear here.[2] We are grateful to all those who considered our request.

The book is divided into two parts. The first consists of essays from women who won the Marty between 1937 and 1958. They include recollections of war-time work in the Canadian atomic research effort and the Wartime Prices and Trade Board, scientific work undertaken in Dr Hans Selye's early pain laboratory and in cytology on the eve of the discovery of DNA. There are accounts by two literary scholars of their searches for manuscripts in post-war France and England.

In the second half of the collection are writings by more recent Marty winners, those who received the award between 1959 and 1987. These include descriptions of the contemporary quest to become and be playwright and painter. The academic manifestation of youth unemployment is depicted by tramping researchers confined to short-term contract work. Here also are first-hand reports from a new frontier in women's lives in scholarship, by women who with the help of the Marty returned to academic studies after other careers and years raising children.

These are hopeful sagas written by optimistic travellers. They chart the faith and support which made prodigious achievement possible, the parents who insisted that both their daughters and sons attend university and reorganized their households, sometimes radically, to ensure this was the case; the teachers and administrators who demanded that young women consider for themselves roles which the wider society named as dangerous and unseemly for their sex; the friends, colleagues and husbands who were happy to step outside traditional gender expectations to smooth the way. They describe the satisfactions of the search, the delight of discovery, the wonderful friendships forged by shared obsessions, the moments of transcendence following months of grey dawns, night terrors and excruciating doubt.

They are also, in their accumulated detail, a telling reply to anyone who might still think, in these closing decades of the twentieth century, that the peculiar gender imbalance in contemporary academic and public life is but an unlucky accident. Here are school girls in northern mining towns in the 1920s and Montreal suburbs in the 1960s struggling to compensate for the stunning oddity of being bright and female. Here are doctoral candidates drawn from three generations contending with supervisors who were sceptical or not much interested, and who had, by shouting matches, brilliant exceptionalism and quiet subterfuge, to be convinced that fine students, even if they were female, might be worth the time. If the nepotism rules and the conventions that women teach only in women's colleges have faded away, the forces directing women toward teaching rather than research and marginal rather than tenured academic posts have not.

Dr Eleanor Clarke Hay, who won the Marty in 1941, wisely observes that 'chosen physical, mental and emotional commitment is the essence of a free life.' These essays are rich with the rewards of commitment, not only to scholarship and art, but to religious faith, marriage and motherhood. Their authors recount the arduous pleasures of bearing and raising children and sustaining families in an uncertain world while trying all the while to write and paint and lead committed public lives. Their reflections make the conclusion of Dr E. Jane Wright, who won the Marty in 1984, all the more compelling. 'It is a sad commentary on our times that, in general, marriage assists men, but retards women in their careers.' The commitment to scholarship still has fearsome personal costs for women which it does not have for men.

Women from the First Wave of Canadian feminists founded the Marty Memorial Scholarship to honour two of their own. We have tried to keep good faith with their traditions, but we still have much to do.

This book is a work of many hands. The project began with Jean Royce, who closely followed the careers of the Marty Scholars and hoped one day to record their stories. She encouraged Lin Buckland to take up this task. On Lin's urging the Marty committee established the working group which became the cheerfully indefatigable editorial board for this book. Without these women, Elspeth Baugh, Lin Buckland, Margaret Gibson, Margaret Hooey and Donna Lounsbury, the project would have been difficult. Together, we were a happy complement of talents and temperaments, and the work became a source of strength and satisfaction. The final drafts of the script were typed and proofed quickly and with great care by Joy Hoselton and Olive Blaney and skillfully copy-edited by Jill Harris. Throughout we have been sustained by the enthusiasm of the Marty Scholars and the support and encouragement of Principal David Smith. Chancellor Agnes M. Benidickson has been our silent partner. It was she who provided the material means to bring to print the project Jean Royce began.

1 Margaret Gillett and Kay Sibbald, *A Fair Shake: autobiographical essays of women at McGill*, Montreal: Eden Press, 1984.
2 All of the replies to our inquiries can be consulted in the Marty Memorial Anniversary Collection at the Queen's University Archives.

The Marty Scholarship – an informal history

MARGARET HOOEY

A Queen's University calendar entry, in 1937, under the heading 'Fellowships Not Controlled by the University,' announced that 'a scholarship valued at not less than $750 was being offered by the Queen's University Alumnae Association to a "woman graduate of Queen's University with a Master's Degree, for a year's graduate work overseas."' With the continued interest and support of graduates and friends of Queen's, the Marty, now valued at $10,000, and advertised today to support an endeavour 'which contributes to the advancement of knowledge, contributes to society, or allows creative expression,' has for 50 years held a unique position among opportunities and honours available to women scholars in Canada. The holders of the award collectively represent a truly outstanding group of women scholars, many of them pioneers in their field, who have distinguished themselves in a wide variety of activities all over the world.

The 50th anniversary of the Marty Scholarship is an appropriate time to pause and reflect on the Scholarship itself, and on the foresight of the women of Queen's University who established it, in 1937, to encourage Queen's women to do graduate study and research. This book celebrates those remarkable pioneers and the equally remarkable scholarship winners.

To understand why the Marty is such an important part of the history of Queen's women, we must look back to 1900 when women graduates began, in an organized fashion (despite a lack of encouragement from the predominantly male 'establishment'!) to try to smooth the way for succeeding generations of women students. At that time Dr Elizabeth Shortt led an independent and determined alumnae group to provide residence space for women students. They began by leasing a furnished house at 64 William Street in Kingston, then rented and furnished the

◁ Aletta Elise Marty.
CREDIT: Kenneth Forbes, RCA.

'Hen Coop' at Clergy and Earl Streets. The need for space grew, and, in 1911, Aletta Marty organized an Alumnae Association with the goal of raising $50,000 to provide a residence. Although the Board of Trustees regularly resisted the women's efforts, their resolve remained firm. Wartime inflation raised the cost of the residence to $160,000 in 1919, but, finally, the Board of Trustees agreed to provide a matching sum if the women provided half the required amount. Through hard work and business acumen they did so by 1923, and the Board authorized construction.

Many battles remained to be fought. In a confident report following a meeting between the Alumnae Executive and the Board of Trustees, Aletta Marty described the delegation as a 'young phalanx to make glad the hearts of those who long had toiled.'[1] Under their pressure, the Board agreed, although not without protest, to leave the administration and management of the residence up to the alumnae.

Charlotte Whitton, later a member of the Board of Trustees, who served on the original residence administration committee, tells the story with her characteristic colour and passion:

The Trustees were satisfied that the Residence would be 'a white elephant, away over on University Avenue with rooming areas traditionally elsewhere,' that money would be lost in the operation .... The Registrar and Treasurer blandly proposed that the Alumnae Association should agree to underwriting the annual deficit. The Alumnae in cold rage asked for a black and white record that 'the Alumnae Association would not be expected to pay interest on the University's contribution' and argued that with proper management the Residence would yield a surplus.[2]

In the half century that followed, the women graduates of Queen's continued to run the residences, operating them so efficiently that, as the Alumnae had predicted, a substantial surplus of funds was accumulated. In 1974, when it appeared that residence accommodation was adequate, the women decided that rather than use the money for 'bricks and mortar' they would set up a facility to encourage continuing education for women – the Ban Righ Foundation. The Foundation is under the control of the Ban Righ Board, the body that for so many years had operated the Women's Residences effectively, independently and profitably.

Mary Alice Murray, a lawyer and Secretary of the Faculty of Law at Queen's from 1962 to 1980, satirized relations between the Alumnae and the Board of Trustees, playing upon the similarities between gender roles in the university and in the patriarchal household:

The husband has left the internal management of the 'house' to the wife, has permitted her a free hand with the house-keeping money (which he has not provided) and has kept aside housekeeping (or budget) surpluses strictly for future plans of hers regarding 'the house.' However he has had the 'household' accounts checked by his auditor. He has held title to the real property, although the wife brought her dower to it (– the analogy seems to fail in the Dower Right of the wife, although they are domiciled in Ontario). He has made the big decisions, more often in consultation with the wife (e.g. the appointing of a 'Nanny' and major alterations and additions to the property).[3]

The pioneer alumnae were also concerned about women students' academic fortunes after they left Queen's. Until 1920 the University did not give financial assistance to students to undertake advanced studies. While the Board of Trustees was proposing 'a number of Fellowships or Scholarships to assist men engaged in graduate studies,' the Alumnae Association was talking about the importance of encouraging women graduates to do graduate work and research 'in centres where the best instruction in their fields is available.'[4] Dr Wilhelmina Gordon, a professor of English at Queen's, urged the Association to set up a travelling scholarship for women graduates, and the Alumnae suggested to the University that it use one of its graduate scholarships for this purpose. The University Scholarship Committee turned down the idea on the grounds that it was discriminatory! The Alumnae Association, spurred into going it alone, proceeded to set up a Scholarship as a memorial to Dr Aletta Marty and her sister, Sophie Marty, both ardent advocates of higher education for women.

The changes in the Marty Memorial Scholarship in fifty years have been part of the revolutionary social changes affecting women during this period. In 1937, the year the Marty was first offered, there were no women registered in the professional programs in the University. All women students were in the Arts Faculty, and only a quarter of Queen's graduates that year were women. Today, half the full-time students of the University are women. Particularly significant are the statistics for the traditional male bastions. In the School of Business, over 50% of students are women; in Law, 38%; Medicine, 36%; Engineering, more than 17%; and more than one-third of the full-time graduate students are women.

Over the years, the terms of the Marty have been broadened to encourage women to pursue new roles and opportunities. In the early years the award was given to young women with MA's studying for degrees in traditional fields. In the last fifteen years, the recipients have included women between the ages of 22 and 45 doing 'a year of study or research,' among them a playwright, a lawyer, an artist, and a concert pianist, as well as those from the more traditional scholarly disciplines.

Changes in the Marty also took into account the coming of age of Canadian universities. For several decades, winners of the Marty were required to study outside Canada. However, in a report to the Committee in 1968, Jean Royce, then Registrar of Queen's, noted the growth of Canadian graduate institutions and argued that 'if a student is to sit under a professor whose output has challenged her' she should be free to do so whether in Canada or abroad. The terms accordingly were revised to permit study anywhere, including Canada.

The Alumnae's two major enterprises of the first half of this century – the building and running of residences, and the setting up and maintaining of a valuable award for women graduates – were inspired by similar motives and supported by a common core of alumnae. The vision and determination these women showed in establishing the Marty have been maintained through the years, as the alumnae of the University adapted the award to emerging needs. The Marty has thus retained its initial freshness and innovative character – a true reflection of the character of the women after whom it was named.

Two names stand out in connection with the Marty: Aletta Marty herself, leader and educator – and Jean Royce, visionary and administrator, for whom a second award for women graduates has now been named.

Aletta Marty holds a special place both in the annals of Canadian education and in the history of the remarkable achievements of women graduates of Queen's University in the first quarter of this century. Born in Mitchell, Ontario, in 1865, she was the youngest of seven children of Swiss parents. As was the pattern with many leaders of Queen's, including Principal John Deutsch and Registrar Jean Royce, Aletta Marty began her university studies by correspondence courses. She taught public school by day and studied at night. Eventually she was able to attend Queen's as a full-time student, graduating in 1894 with an MA and the University Medal in modern languages. In 1919, after 25 years of teaching French and German in St Thomas and Ottawa high schools, she was named Inspector of Public Schools in Toronto – the first woman to hold this position in Ontario. In the same year, Queen's University gave her an honorary degree of Doctor of Laws, the first Canadian woman so honoured.

'Dr Marty was ever ready to struggle for the rights of her sex in order that life itself might be the richer, and that literature, art, education and social conditions might reap the benefit of women's intellectual and emotional influence.'[5] She was a zealous scholar, a woman who spent her vacations in educational work. She wrote and edited a number of textbooks used in schools throughout the Province. In a bold interpretation of what was legitimate classroom activity she fought successfully for the introduction of experimental new methods – such as use of films and gramophones. Her book, *Creative Young Canada*, a collection of original verse, drawings and musical compositions, demonstrates her emphasis on the importance of creative expression in the educational process. Her reports to the Toronto Board of Education were said to be 'crowded with innovations.'[6]

Aletta Marty and her sister Sophie, also an outstanding language scholar and graduate of Queen's, were extremely close. Sophie, who headed the Department of Modern Languages at Stratford Collegiate, collaborated with Aletta in editing a French primer for schools in Ontario. Sophie was a staunch supporter of Aletta in all her undertakings and was with Aletta in South Africa when Aletta, doing a year's inspectorship there, died suddenly from a heart attack. The shock was too great for her sister; Sophie herself died on the homeward journey.

Aletta Marty's qualities of confidence and leadership had been critical factors inspiring the women graduates of Queen's to build residences and encourage women to do graduate studies. She believed strongly in equal opportunity for women. A tribute in the *Alumnae News* in 1929 affirmed her belief in women's capacities:

She maintained that there is no sex in brains, ability or character, that a woman dowered by nature with certain gifts should be as free to use them as a man, and should be able to decide for herself and not on account of economic necessity where her path in life should lie.[7]

The Marty grew in prestige and importance because, for over 30 years, it was nurtured and administered by the particular genius of Jean Royce. As Registrar, Jean Royce was known to have a 'built-in geiger counter for detecting able and eager students'[8] – both men and women. Not only did she have an uncanny ability to identify promise, often quite hidden from parents and other observers, but she was able to change permanently a student's self image and confidence. Generations of young people were influenced by her own excitement about learning and her belief that there need be no impediments to the full realization of potential. One Marty scholar, now a consulting geologist, wrote, in a personal letter:

Jean Royce.
CREDIT: Ashley and Crippen.

I shall never forget that day in your office at Queen's when, in a meeting with you, you suddenly leaned across your desk and said, 'Esther, what do you *really* want to do?' And, in your manner of asking, conveyed to me that I could be whatever I wanted to be and do whatever I wanted to do. And, for the first time in my life, I felt that the whole world was in my hands.

Jean Royce also had first-hand knowledge of promising women scholars across the country because of her position as Convenor of the Fellowship Committee of the Canadian Federation of University Women and Convenor of the Standards Committee of the International Federation of University Women. She sought out eligible Queen's graduates, wherever they were, to tell them about the Marty and personally to encourage them to apply.

As administrator of the University's awards systems, Jean Royce knew exactly what it took to keep an award financially competitive. She advised the Alumnae Association when the capital fund for the Marty needed a 'boost' by a campaign for funds and, working with the Association, maintained the selection committee as a committed, vibrant group. At key points she encouraged the broadening of terms to keep the award current with changing trends in education and society. Indeed, her vision of the power and the meaning of the Marty inspired this book.

1 Charlotte Whitton, 'Seasmhachd Oil Thigh Na Banrighinn,' *Queen's Review*, Vol. 22, No. 7, October 1948, p.184.
2 Charlotte Whitton, 'Ban Righ Hall – How It Came To Be,' *Queen's University Alumnae Association 1900-1961 and Women's Residences at Queen's*, mimeo, p.25.
3 Mary Alice Murray, letter to Dr J.A. Corry, re Constitution of Ban Righ Board, *Ban Righ Board: Consolidation of Material Relating to the History of the Authority for and the Administration of Women's Residences at Queen's*, mimeo, 1963.
4 Mary White, 'The Marty Memorial Scholarship 1937-1947,' *The Queen's Review*, Vol. 21, No. 9, December 1947, p.247.
5 Miss Elsie Pomeroy, 'Aletta E. Marty: An Appreciation,' *The Queen's Review*, January 1933, p.4.
6 Donald Jones, 'Aletta Marty fought the battle for art courses in high school,' *Toronto Star*, October 15, 1983, p.16.
7 Jessie Muir, *Alumnae News*, Vol. XII, December 1929, p.52.
8 Excerpt from Principal Corry's citation at the awarding of her honorary degree of Doctor of Laws on November 8, 1968.

Part One

1937–1958

By choice and by chance

JEANNE LE CAINE AGNEW

I was born in Port Arthur, Ontario. The city has since been renamed; the beautiful house in which I was born has been turned into a duplex; a high-rise apartment house tops the hill down which in the winter I used to slide on my piece of cardboard on the way to Central School. Still when I drive up Arthur Street (now called Red River Road) and see old Central School, Trinity United Church, and Port Arthur Collegiate Institute, I know that I am home, and that whatever it is called, this city, like me, remains at heart Canadian.

My father and mother came to Port Arthur as newlyweds about 1910. It was a marriage of opposites. My mother, born and raised in Southern Ontario, was a good student and longed to go to university, but financial problems made it necessary for her to go instead to Saskatchewan to teach. My father moved from Ontario to Saskatchewan at the age of five and had very little formal education, spending his time helping on the farm in spring, summer, and fall, and snow-bound in the winter. Nevertheless, he too valued education, read a great deal and remembered what he read. In his early twenties he left the farm, took a night course in electricity, and spent the major part of his life as electrician for the Saskatchewan Pool Elevators in Port Arthur.

Mother was vivacious, lively, out-going and involved, especially in church-related activities. Dad was quiet, reserved, loved the out-of-doors, and found social occasions an ordeal. In the present day they might have gone separate ways as 'incompatible.' Fortunately for me they created a compromise which gave our family the best of both worlds. My earliest memories are fishing expeditions in a small motorboat that Dad created by rebuilding a wrecked sailboat and inserting a motor he found in a junk pile. When I was six he built a small cottage on what is now Mackenzie Beach, on Lake Superior, about 17 miles north of the city. At first we could reach it only by boat or rail. We were not even allowed to buy the land.

Jeanne Le Caine Agnew.

Now it is available by road. Summer cottages and even permanent homes have grown up not far from us. But we have been able to buy enough land to maintain our privacy, and the beauty remains. For sixty-three years this spot has, more than any other, been the well-spring of my life.

Our no-frills life style was rich in relationships with each other and with the world around us. I grew up with two firm convictions: I would some day be a mother and I intended to be a teacher. During a blueberry picking expedition near Nipigon I picked out the school I would teach at – an attractive little one-room country school near the Nipigon River.

At last I was 17, had completed Grade 13 and in addition two years at the Technical High School, and Queen's was willing to accept me. I chose Queen's mostly because one of my favorite teachers had graduated there. My brother had already demonstrated that he was 'a genius' so my father decreed that he should be the one to go to Queen's since it was clearly not possible to support two in college. Mother had different ideas. She was firmly of the 'both or neither' opinion, and came up with the financing plan which involved leaving Dad at home during the school year and setting up housekeeping in Kingston for the rest of us (mother, my brother, my nine-year-old sister, and me.)

And so in the fall of 1934 we descended on Kingston. We were unprepared for Kingston's venerable beauty – the impressive old buildings, the big spreading trees, the narrow streets, historic Fort Henry, and the strip of park right on the water's edge with no railroads or grain elevators to separate the city proper from the lake front. We felt we ought to speak in hushed voices and wondered if we would ever be accepted there. The warmth and hospitality of the people of Kingston, and especially of the University community, soon dispelled our doubts. Before a month had passed my brother was leading the traditional pre-game parade, a snaky line of pyjama-clad freshman, he carrying a candle which enthusiastic upperclassmen were valiantly attempting to keep lighted.

Queen's had an academic policy then which was very helpful to me. In the first year of the Arts curriculum we had little choice. We took a subject from each prescribed area. I found myself in calculus, English, political science, economics, and psychology. Each of my professors was knowledgeable, concerned, articulate and demanding. At the end of the first year I had decided to major in mathematics, and after much consideration to minor in economics.

That decision was almost altered after I took the economics final. I thought I had studied for it, but I felt that my answers to the various questions were completely inadequate. Imagine my surprise when I learned at the end of the summer that I had been given the prize for the highest grade in the course. The prize had an impressive name and a monetary value of $21. That prize did a great deal for me. It let me realize that I could handle courses in university (even in areas other than mathematics). It helped me understand that the inadequacy of my answers came in part from my lack of understanding, and in part also from the complexity of the entire field. It made me see the importance of tangible recognition of academic excellence. I resolved that when I became a teacher I would try to establish awards for academic excellence even if they had to be small. Mother insisted that the $21 be deposited in an account to pay for my postgraduate education. Thus, I gave up the idea of the little school at Nipigon and decided I would teach in a high school somewhere in Northern Ontario.

I cannot say enough about the supportive nature of the Queen's community: the Registrar, Miss Jean Royce, the heart of the University, who knew us all by name, and was never too busy to talk to us; Dean Matheson, who gave me wise counsel and his personal autographed copy of Osgood's calculus book; Dr Mackintosh, who had his economics seminars meet in his home; Dr Knox, who may have unconsciously become a role model for me, since his demanding teaching covered a real concern that we learn. My fellow students were all male, with the exception of Hilda Merkley. They accepted us in the spirit of friendly competition, always ready to compare notes, rejoice in successes, and discuss difficult concepts.

The most important influence on my life during those years was Dr Norman Miller, my advisor and friend. He encouraged me and cautioned me, praised me and criticized me, introduced me to the wonders and excitement of mathematics and also to its difficulties and challenges. He and his wife welcomed me into their home and so began a life-long friendship.

Each summer I spent some time at 'the cottage' on Lake Superior to assimilate what I had learned, to drink deeply of the peace and beauty of the solid granite rocks, the slender white birch trees, and the sparkling water. I thought about the wonders of mathematics, limitless avenues of exploration that I had not dreamed existed. In Grade 5 my teacher had written home, after I had scored 20% on an arithmetic exam, 'This child is good in English but hopeless in Mathematics.' In high school I had found the ordered discipline of less computational mathematics both easy and satisfying. At Queen's I began to see that mathematics held tremendous potential for excitement. Was I really equal to taking off in this unknown direction? Perhaps I might even teach at the college level!

I managed to compress the four years required for a BA into three so that I had a fourth year to obtain a master's degree. What to do then? My family and my professors encouraged me to apply to various schools and attempt to get financial assistance. It was Dr Miller who suggested that I apply at Harvard, his alma mater, though for me it would have to be Radcliffe. I was accepted there (and at other schools) and given a scholarship that would cover tuition. Great, but not enough. It was then that someone made the audacious suggestion that I apply for the Marty Memorial Scholarship. I felt undeserving when I applied, and even more so when I gathered with the finalists for the personal interview and tea presided over by Dr Hilda Laird. What a delightful person she was and how I wished that I had her poise and elegance! I wished that there were enough money to give the award to all of us. I hope that for them it did not mean the difference between ending and beginning. Fortunately for me I was the lucky one. I felt honored, grateful, inadequate, and a little scared.

Harvard was ostensibly an all-male school. I lived in a Radcliffe graduate dormitory; I enrolled at Radcliffe; I wrote my exams at Longfellow Hall at Radcliffe; and I graduated in the Radcliffe ceremony at Sanders Theater. But everything else I did at Harvard. My mathematics classes were in Sever Hall; I studied in Widener Library; all my professors were Harvard professors; and my fellow students were all Harvard men, with the exception of Anne O'Neill. We felt in every way like Harvard students.

During the first year I had a course in Complex Variables under Dr G.D. Birkhoff. It was obvious that he was indeed what he was reported to be, one of the greatest American-born mathematicians. He was also able to convey the excitement of his subject. We might have to go back over the lecture notes to fill in some details, but that was unimportant compared to the insight he was able to give us. True to my first decision, I also took a course in mathematical economics from Professor Leontief, who later became famous in that field. Although I found it interesting and valued the opportunity to study with him, I decided that my first love was mathematics, that I would like to proceed to a PhD and perhaps even have Dr Birkhoff for my major advisor.

Dr Birkhoff accepted me but not without some slight hesitation – yes, because I was a female. His previous female advisee had married and become the mother of five children. I do not know whether or not she later used her mathematics in any way, but apparently it was his opinion that she had wasted time which he otherwise might have spent with some more mathematically productive student. In the present climate I should have been angered at this discriminatory attitude. I am ashamed to say it did not occur to me to be angry. He was a good advisor, hard-working and encouraging and, most unusual, prompt in responding to questions and in returning potential pieces of my dissertation.

The dissertation took shape for the most part at the cottage on Thunder Bay, an ideal place to think and create. Sometimes it moved quickly and sometimes at such a snail's pace that I feared I had gotten into the wrong business entirely. I had promised to write Dr Birkhoff reporting on my progress, and it seemed to me I had nothing to say. I did write him, telling him what little I had been able to invent, and then commenting on the difficulty I was having trying to operate the old motorboat that my father had made in my early childhood. I received his reply almost by return mail, making encouraging comments about my ideas and then giving me a long account of his experiences one summer with a recalcitrant motorboat.

My time at Harvard-Radcliffe went quickly. During my second year I was funded by the Canadian Federation of University Women's Travelling Fellowship and later by awards from Radcliffe and some part-time work. It was clear to me now that I wanted most of all to be a college or university teacher, and I hoped that when I became one I could maintain the atmosphere of friendship and respect which characterized the professor-student relationship both at Queen's and at Harvard. I graduated (at the Radcliffe ceremony) in 1941.

In the fall of 1941 I began my first teaching job, as an instructor at Smith College, a beautiful college with excellent academic standards. I taught trigonometry and calculus, and a reading course involving two graduate students. I had an apartment as faculty resident in one of the dormitories. For the first time in my life I was in a completely female environment. It should have been perfect.

Life was not without its complications, however. The most pleasant one took place in 1938 on my first Sunday in Cambridge, when I met, at church, a young student beginning his work toward a PhD in History. Our friendship developed into love, and four and a half years later, December 25, 1942, we were married. The unusual date was the outcome of the major complication for every person during those years, the beginning and the escalation of World War II. He had postponed the completion of his graduate education to enlist as an Ensign in the Supply Corps of the US

Navy. A few days after our marriage he was sent to duty in Hawaii, where he remained for 27 months.

During my years at Radcliffe, and especially during my year at Smith College, I became increasingly conscious of the fact that I was a Canadian, and proud to be one; that my country was engaged in a devastating, thankless, yet necessary war; that it had supported me in my years of need and helped me get the education I so much cherished; and therefore that I ought to be doing my share in the war in which Canada was so deeply involved. I left Smith to work for the National Research Council, and was soon sent to Montreal to be a part of the Canadian branch of the Atomic Research Effort.

Like everyone else who was involved in this project, I think often of the way our work has been used, and ask myself whether I would make the same decision again. Given the situation of 1943 there was no other decision that could be made. The discovery of the laws of the Universe has been our assignment since the beginning of time. The secrets of the atom are a part of this body of knowledge. Before World War II began, the study of atomic energy was well advanced in several countries. There was no way it could be stopped, only a way to hope it could be controlled by responsible people. There are many pieces of knowledge that have great potential for both good and evil. Beginning with the discovery of fire and moving ahead to television and the invasion of space, each advance carries with it the ability to help or harm. Even books are not exempt. It remains for society to take the responsibility to see that the correct choices are made. In Pogo's famous line, 'We have seen the enemy and they is us.'

In Montreal I was assigned to share an office with a Canadian physicist, Dr Carson Mark, who later went to Los Alamos and became head of the atomic project there. He advised me and encouraged me in my work, and allowed me to share with his delightful family (an amazingly cheerful and competent wife and three pre-school children) in the seasonal celebrations which would otherwise have been quite lonely for me. I was surer than ever that some day I would teach *and* be a mother.

After my husband returned, we spent a couple of years at Harvard while he began work on his dissertation. Finally, with the promise of a teaching job for my husband, we set out for Oklahoma in our 1934 Chevrolet.

Stillwater, Oklahoma, was quite a change from Port Arthur, or Kingston, or Montreal, or Cambridge. It was rather flat and quite hot. The 'college courts' turned out to be recycled army housing, and the attractive older brick buildings on campus were supplemented by ugly quonset huts. One of these quonsets housed the Mathematics Department.

Lt. Agnew and wife reunited after 27 months. May 1945.

When our first child died shortly after birth, the Mathematics Department invited me to teach, and thus began an association that lasted more than forty years.

Postwar unrest hit Oklahoma as well. The legislature required any one working for the University to sign an oath of allegiance. I was still a Canadian and this posed a problem. Moreover, the state had a nepotism rule. But there was an influx of students returning to school on the GI Bill, and a great lack of qualified teachers, especially in mathematics. The loyalty oath was modified to accommodate foreigners. The new head of the Department of Mathematics persuaded the regents to set aside the nepotism rule so that I could be offered a tenure-track teaching position. He pointed out to me the great need for qualified teachers and set down the ground rules: I would never be assigned a class before 9 am or after 3 pm; the family would always take precedence over school should a conflict of demands arise. My widowed mother-in-law, who was visiting to welcome our third child, agreed to stay a year to take care of the family. So here I was being offered my two greatest desires on a silver platter. I decided that I would try juggling the needs of family and teaching, and I have never regretted the decision.

And so began a succession of delightful years. The family increased to five. I loved teaching, and threw myself into it whole-heartedly. In the Mathematics Department, we each taught fifteen hours a week, and after the children were in bed I still had papers to grade. The courses I taught were primarily graduate level courses, since many of the staff at that time did not have PhD degrees. That in itself required preparation time, but it was extremely interesting. I felt myself challenged and challenged my students in turn. Oklahoma Agricultural and Mechanical College became Oklahoma State University, and the graduate program became more demanding. The quonsets were removed, the campus was beautified, the people were friendly and accepting. We bought a house and began to call Stillwater 'home.'

Meanwhile the family blossomed. I managed to get a reliable older woman who came in at 8:30 and stayed till 4:00 to run the ship. She had a no-nonsense way of handling the children, and they thrived under it. Yet she was sympathetic with their problems and ready to greet the older ones when they returned from school. Sometimes I met my classes in my Den Mother's uniform. Sometimes a pre-school Agnew attended a class in American History or Advanced Calculus. Just outside my classroom window the University pre-school had its playground. I could glance out and see the current four-year-old Agnew playing in a carefully supervised situation, and I thought, 'How can I be so lucky!'

When it became clear that Oklahoma was to become my home, and that I was a foreigner in my own family, I somewhat reluctantly took out American citizenship. But every summer, even if it was only for two or three weeks, we packed up bag and baggage and headed north for the Lake Superior cottage, anxious for the magic moment when the car would stop, the door open. Then five children, one dog, and two parents would make a concerted rush to the lake shore to see how the intervening year had changed the shoreline, what treasures the waves had washed up or stolen away, whether the inevitable uninvited visitors had broken windows or had left the cottage livable. So what if there was no electricity, no telephone, no running water, wood to cut, mosquitoes to avoid. There was the smell of fresh clean air, the rich green of the forest and the shining white of the birch trees, rafts to build, special hideaways to seek out, raspberries and blueberries to pick, the cliff to explore, and the big beautiful moon rising above the water, making a shimmering silver streak to follow in rowboat or canoe.

I cannot say enough about the men in my life during the teaching-parenting years. Most important was my husband, who did his share and more in the care and counselling of the children from birth through adolescence. Of course we made mistakes but we made them jointly and with the best of intentions in the spirit of love. He was more than supportive of my involvement at the University, he was enthusiastic about it. Whenever possible he encouraged me to take on student and faculty responsibilities, and was always willing to share in them. His own activities as a Professor of History and a dedicated and active member of the United Methodist Church enriched the life of the entire family.

My male colleagues counselled me, helped me, and encouraged me in my work and could be counted on to entertain any children required to wait a bit while I worked with students. The graduate student advisor, aware of the graduate theses I had been directing in Number Theory, pointed out to me that these topics would make a good book in Number Theory. And so, after several years of work, *Explorations in Number Theory* was born. It was not a money-maker since number theory was at that time somewhat out of favor. But it was an extremely satisfying book to me. I dedicated it to my doctoral students, and used for the cover a picture of Ouimet Canyon, one of the natural partially explored wonders of Northern Ontario not far from Thunder Bay.

12

Nothing remains the same. Our children grew and, as they should, they have moved into lives of their own. The 'empty nest' was not nearly as traumatic as I had been led to expect. However, added to decreasing needs at home was a change in my academic situation. The supply of graduates with PhD degrees in mathematics had increased enormously since the postwar days of shortage. The increased funding for higher education as the economy improved meant that we could now hire more and better-prepared faculty. We had an influx of bright young men, fresh from more or less prestigious institutions, who were anxious to teach graduate courses and work with graduate students. I was willing to move over and alter the nature of my professional activities.

Again chance stepped in and took a hand. Our new department head decided we should send out a newsletter to our graduates in order to maintain contact with them. Quite unexpected was the spin-off which resulted from a question on the response sheet: 'Did your education at Oklahoma State University prepare you for your present position?' Those graduates engaged in teaching replied with a resounding yes. From those who had taken jobs in industry the response was no. The comment 'I wish I had had a chance to see my mathematics put to use in real-world situations' was one with which I heartily agreed. As a result, a colleague and I (funded by the National Science Foundation) created a course in which persons working in industry came to campus and presented problems they had encountered and which involved only undergraduate mathematics. The class then searched the literature, developed a solution, refined and tested it, and wrote a technical report.

The project grew to involve lectures by television to in-state institutions. Written versions of the problems were made available nation-wide. Joined by two other colleagues, we revised the project and TEAM was born, 'Teaching Experiential Applied Mathematics.' This created learning modules consisting of on-site video, written Resource Books, and computer software, all distributed free of charge to colleges, community colleges, and universities in the United States and Canada.

It seemed valuable to introduce the computer and some real applications into the teaching of undergraduate linear algebra. *Linear Algebra with Applications* was published in 1978, the second edition in 1983, and my co-author and I are currently preparing the third edition.

Two years ago my husband and I retired from active teaching. At least that is our official status, professor emeritus. This does have advantages. We can take off in February for a trip to Singapore to visit our son. We can be present when needed to help in an emergency or take part in a celebration. Best of all we do not need to return to Oklahoma during the 103-degree days of the end of August just because the semester is beginning, but can enjoy the cool breezes of Lake Superior at least until the first home football game.

However, we are not as free from professional activities as many envision. I remember the Finnish couple who lived next door to us in Port Arthur – 'Old Mama, Old Papa, sitting on the porch in the rocker.' This description does not apply to us. My colleague and I are now working on AIM, 'Applications in Mathematics,' a grant to create learning modules based on real problems from industry, this time for high school. He is in charge of video, and I am in charge of writing and computer software. I hope that our material will reach the high school in Northern Ontario where I never managed to teach.

I hope that the mathematics world is better than I found it, if not by some previously undiscovered theorem at least by some inspired students. Perhaps Dr Aletta Marty, as the first woman inspector of Ontario schools and a crusader for art courses in high schools, would be willing to accept AIM as an effort to encourage in high schools the art of problem solving.

What are we doing here?

ANNE HARLEY SEDGEWICK CARVER

It is a sunny August day and I am writing at a table set in the wide open doors of our Nova Scotia barn. In front of me is the house, white painted with apple green gable ends, sitting serenely in the curving sweep of freshly mown, very green grass.

We face out across more rolling fields full of wild flowers, studded here and there with a dark spruce tree or two, towards Port Joli Bay, the Atlantic Ocean and eventually, one supposes, Portugal. Today the house is comfortably anchored into the landscape by a clothes line on which my daughter Deborah's and my small grandson's clean laundry is sporting in the light sea breeze. By a happy chance all their garments are blue, green, pale yellow and white, with only the merest touch of red (a diminutive pair of Benjamin's socks) and on the ground there are one blue and two yellow pails.

A hundred or so swallows are darting and soaring and swooping across my view. This year's fledglings are being chivied by their parents, with a barrage of twittering, to practise up their aerobatics for the long flight south. Now and then they alight for a breather on the telephone and hydro wires, but at some mysterious signal they are all off in a flash to circle and dive bomb again. The swallows leave early. They will all be gone at the end of August.

Off to my right, across a couple of hundred yards of Queen Anne's lace, wild roses, vetch and ancient apple trees, is our other much older house. We are a small company here at the moment but our second daughter, Jenny, and her husband and their friends will soon join us and after that our son, Peter, and his family. That will fill up both houses.

This barn is now a people place, domestic animals long forgotten. It was transformed into respectability four years ago so that a hundred guests could sit down to the wedding breakfast when our Debby was married. No ordinary marquee could be counted on to stand up against our

Anne Harley Sedgewick Carver.

hurricane-strength August winds. I will be seventy-two years old two weeks from today and in the evening there will be long tables set out here for twenty or thirty relatives and neighbours, with a glowing red lobster at each place, and great bowls of potato salad and green salad, brown bread and butter and birthday cake. My birthday is an annual excuse for a lobster feast. There was even one year when a male guest with unexpected talents created a somewhat threatening cake shaped like a lobster.

This morning Humphrey and I awoke with the sunlight pouring in through our eastern windows and were gathering our energies and resources to meet another day when Hump asked, out of the blue, 'What are we doing here?' He did not mean 'Why aren't we up and getting the breakfast?' He was, rather, asking a philosophical question which could have set rolling hours of pleasant ruminating, discursive examination of past aspirations, plans, tastes, the foreseeable and unforeseen twists of fortune that brought us to this moment. But there was a helter skelter of little running feet, and the radiant face of small Benjamin appeared over the end of the bed. Life at once became immediate, here and now, no time for contemplation.

I confess at once that I have never been much given to self-examination. Normally it seems a waste of time. There are so many demands for one's interest, attention and action. So often the equivalent of my grandson's shining morning face snatches one from self to other. However, the historical reasons for being here at Port Joli are straight-forward enough. I was born in Toronto and have lived all my life in Ontario with the exception of important departures for the purpose of education and vacation; but my parents were born in Nova Scotia, and my forebears have lived and died here for six generations on my mother's side, and four on my father's. The roots are deep, and Nova Scotia has always held a large piece of my heart.

In 1902 my mother, Molly Robertson, then twenty-four years old, persuaded my grandfather to build a summer cottage in Shelburne County at the point where Bloody Creek runs into the Clyde River and the two flow out seven miles to the sea. My grandfather was born not far from there in Barrington Passage and had gone as a youth to Halifax to seek his fortune. He did very well in the hardware and ship's chandlery business, and his shop on the Halifax waterfront has now been preserved as a part of the Nova Scotia Maritime Museum. He built the cottage on the Clyde which he called 'Struan' after the Perthshire centre of the Robertson clan. It is an ultra-simple, stripped down, three storey structure of no architectural merit, but to all succeeding generations Struan has been next thing to Paradise. I was there first when I was just short of one year old. It was at Struan that we met our beloved Nova Scotia uncles and aunts and cousins. It was there that we first experienced the glories of the ocean, salt and sand and beaches. We learned to swim, to paddle our own canoes, to handle them over the rapids, to light a picnic fire, to camp and to tempt a trout with a fly with a romantic name – Parmachene Belle, or Jenny Lind, or Silver Doctor.

Humphrey and I bought our Port Joli property, only fifty miles away, because it seemed important to me that our children and our nephews and nieces and all their families should have an opportunity to know each other. Struan has the interior of Nova Scotia and the lovely wilderness rivers flowing from it, as well as a choice of beaches not too far away. Here at Port Joli we have the sea and a spectacular wilderness sand beach on our very door step, and as well miles of rocky coast to explore.

Though my father loved Nova Scotia and was probably at his happiest at Struan with a fly rod in his hand, the Sedgewicks of his generation almost all left Nova Scotia and fanned out across Canada. Great-grandfather Sedgewick was a Presbyterian Minister who in 1849 left his church in Aberdeen and, with his family, came to Middle Musquodoboit in Halifax County. There he stayed until he died. He had thirteen children, of whom my grandfather was the first born in Canada. Great-grandfather graduated in theology from Glasgow University, but it pleases me that he received the degree of Doctor of Divinity from Queen's in 1887, just fifty years before I achieved my BA. His sons included a Moderator of the Presbyterian Church and a Justice of the Supreme Court of Canada. My grandfather stayed at home and farmed in Middle Musquodoboit and was not over-burdened with this world's goods. He was a dyed-in-the-wool Conservative, as were all the Sedgewicks, and he ran, unsuccessfully, for a seat in the Nova Scotia Legislative Assembly. His attic was full of back numbers of *Blackwoods Magazine* sent over regularly by a cousin in Scotland. From these my father profited greatly. The Sedgewick family's favourite indoor sport was a ferocious argument on the subjects of politics and religion.

My father put himself through Dalhousie University by teaching in country schools, and when he finally graduated he went off to Toronto to study law at Osgoode Hall. He met my mother when he was a student in Halifax. No one, of course, thought of sending my mother to university. She was sent to London to boarding school, played the violin, adored dancing and was by all accounts both beautiful and witty. She did attend some lectures on English literature given by Professor Archibald MacMechan, who was a family friend.

It interests me that my mother's life at the turn of the century seems to have been much less restricted than social commentators have led us to believe. Perhaps her mother's early death and her father's indulgence account for this. Young men and women, at least when there were several of them, seemed to go off on all kinds of picnics and excursions unencumbered by anyone resembling a chaperone. Mother worked as a volunteer at the North End City Mission on the other side of Halifax and was allowed to walk home alone at night through some of Halifax's seamier slums. She went off to London to buy her trousseau before she was married with only another young woman friend of her own age. On the other hand, she was engaged to my father for eight long years while he was a struggling young lawyer in Toronto. To have married him, gone with him and looked for a job, was not acceptable in 1900. At last they were married, spent their honeymoon at Struan and settled down in Toronto. My sister, Mary, was born in 1912, and I in 1914, two weeks after the outbreak of the Great War.

My childhood was unclouded. Our parents loved us. My mother gave us her full attention and was inventive, full of fun, and appreciative. Nevertheless, outside the family I was a very shy little girl, much dependent on my older sister for support. Where does this ridiculous sensation of personal inadequacy begin, this haunting feeling of not having quite come up to the mark? In spite of my generally optimistic and cheerful temperament it has not entirely gone away with age!

I remember a curious recurrent dream in which, playing in the street in front of our house, I was run over by a steam roller. I picked myself up and found that I was flat like a gingerbread man or a cut-out paper doll. The operator of the steam-roller looked at me without emotion and said, 'It serves you right.'

When I was six years old we moved to a new house at the eastern end of Lonsdale Road. Inside the house were Mum and Dad, my sister Mary and me, Elsie our 'cook-general' and Kim, our Airedale dog. I was old enough now to be fully aware of both people and places. I had, in fact, become recognizably 'me.' This house and these people meant home, and were a strong anchor and support for me all through my school years, even when I was far away from them. Things remained unchanged until my sister married and went to live in India in 1932, and my mother and father and I moved to Ottawa in 1933.

My school career began in Toronto at Bishop Strachan School, just six blocks up Lonsdale Road from where we lived. For nine years I walked there and back every day with my sister and a growing group of friends. For three years more I was away at boarding school in Scotland: St Leonards School in the ancient city of St Andrews, famous for its bloody history, its University, its ghosts, and, of course, golf. Both these schools had been in operation for fifty or sixty years and had more than three hundred pupils.

I loved school. It was popular to say you hated it, but this I never understood. In the nineteen-twenties Bishop Strachan School had many good teachers, perhaps the most noteworthy being the handful of talented women from the British Isles, with degrees from British universities. Our Head Mistress was Miss Harriet Walsh, known to us as 'Hatty.' She had graduated from Trinity College, Dublin, and was a slightly wild Irish woman with a formidable temper but with a keen sense of the dramatic and an unswerving appreciation of excellence. She taught Holy Scripture (it was a High Church Anglican School), and I can see her storming up and down the classroom acting out all the parts at once in the story of the raising of Lazarus or the parable of the foolish virgins, with an intensity and passion worthy of Dublin's Abbey Theatre.

At that time BSS was specially strong in history and English. We did a tremendous amount of written homework which, of course, the teachers had to correct, but the students profited. At St Leonards I remember one of my teachers chiding the class with, 'Here's Anne who comes from Canada, and she writes better English than any of you.' I regretted that she had expected so little of Canada, but I was pleased for my old school. I found myself behind my contemporaries at St Leonards in mathematics and languages – far, far behind in Latin and Greek. Fortunately, there was a high teacher-to-student ratio and I was able to catch up without too much difficulty. In fact, the academic standards at both schools were high. In the private schools I think my generation often was taught by a group of clever women seeking a career, when few were open to them, because many of the men they might have married had been killed in the 1914-1918 war.

The differences in the two schools was in atmosphere and point of view, rather than academics. Bishop Strachan was strongly religious and Anglican. We wore white veils and went to Chapel every morning. While I was a student there the 'new' Chapel was built. We helped with our pennies. The Chapel was, and is, a lovely place. I sang in the choir and loved it dearly. Even the most skeptical young people perhaps absorbed a touch of mystery and wonder there.

Looking back I think BSS put rather more stress than was good for the already over-conscientious on high mindedness, good manners, and general nobility of character. St Leonards was in every way more relaxed, less serious-minded, secular and good humoured. Scripture lessons were exercises in higher criticism, more Northrop Frye than evangelical. It was a great release to me to find that to be teased and laughed at a bit was OK, and usually was the outcome of affection. Doing well at school was as much applauded as excelling at athletics. We played every sort of team game and I was hopeless at all of them, but it did not matter. We walked and picnicked on the cliffs in groups of three or four on school holidays. We swam in the cold North Sea, and played golf on one of the lesser but excellent golf courses. I came back to Nova Scotia in the summer, but at Christmas and Easter my British school friends took me home. It was a great time for growing independence, bolstering self-confidence and great happiness, and out of it all came life-long friends.

There have been very few times in my experience when I have made a decision, consciously and firmly, which was calculated to change the course of my life. I can count them on one hand. My first independent decision of this kind took me to Queen's; my second back to Queen's to graduate studies after my father died suddenly at sixty-one; my third, to abandon my doctoral thesis and go back to Ottawa to a wartime Government job; my fourth was to apply for a permanent position in Government service when the war was over; the fifth was to marry Humphrey and retire.

I came home from school in Scotland a term earlier than had been expected in order to be my sister's bridesmaid at her marriage and to see something of her before she went to India. Then I enrolled at Trinity College with the intention of studying for a BA in English and History with a bit of Greek thrown in. This was not a very serious decision. I was merely following the line I expected myself to follow. I slipped into Trinity without much thought or interest and slipped out again just as easily after one term, when my father, who by this time was a Judge of the Supreme Court of Ontario, was asked by Prime Minister R.B. Bennett to come to Ottawa and head up the new Tariff Board which had been agreed to at the recent Ottawa Imperial Economic Conference. My lack of initiative is puzzling. I had found myself a bit out of step with my old friends in Toronto. Perhaps, like many young people, I needed a fallow period after three years of remarkable independence and activity. I simply went along to Ottawa with my parents. I loved Ottawa and fell in with a delightful group of young people there who made my late teens and early twenties joyful.

In 1934 I made the first major personal independent decision of my life. I would go to Queen's and study Economics and History. The motive for this had been developing slowly. We were concerned with the puzzles of the Depression, the growth of the peace movement, and the interest of the churches in the social gospel. In particular I had talked a good deal with a great friend in England, Cyril Hudson, a Canon of St Alban's Cathedral, who wrote a book called *A Preface to a Christian Sociology* and dedicated it to me. It appeared to me that one could not be the slightest use in looking at the world's problems without knowing a great deal more about economics than I did.

In retrospect my three undergraduate years at Queen's seem cloudless. Principal Fyfe, with his delicious wit, and Principal Wallace with his broad compassion, commanded my admiration and affection. They belonged to the era when university presidents were required, above all, to be scholars. Ban Righ Hall was hospitable. Winnifred Kidd, the new Dean of Women, brought us a breath of the world of affairs with her talk of 'Tony Eden' and other famous people she had met as a delegate to the League of Nations. Her successor, Dr Alice Vibert Douglas, distinguished astral physicist, I came to know much better, and loved her for her clear-eyed integrity, her standards as high as the heavens she knew all about, her optimism and humour and her tolerance of young people with life styles quite different from her own. Jean Royce, that miracle of order and calm efficiency, steered us kindly but firmly through the intricacies of the calendar. Contrary to my experience at Toronto, the atmosphere was one of broad, open choices. Compulsory courses outside of one's chosen field were few. My one required science course was Zoology 1. I enjoyed it so much I might almost have wavered in my choice of specialization. I came top of my class in the final exam, which pleased me greatly.

I had chosen to major in economics with a minor in history. The economics class was at 8 o'clock in the morning and Professor Pete MacQueen, who was substituting for Dr Mackintosh that year, was adept at waking the sleeping giants in the front row with a well aimed piece of chalk, not missing a word of his lecture in the process. At the end of term I was embarrassed to find I had made only fifty marks in the Christmas exam. I was called to the office by Dr Curtis, who persuaded me to switch to a major in history and a minor in economics. This was a blow to pride, but a very good thing in the long run. The minor in economics served me well, while the switch to a heavier involvement in history was in

Anne Harley Sedgewick Carver. Trout fishing up Bloody Creek.

keeping with my past enthusiasms and supported my growing interest in social issues and especially international affairs.

Of course I enjoyed the atmosphere of Queen's. A very great asset was the smallness of Queen's, which made it possible for students, especially Honours students, to get to know their professors. The staff group in economics and political science were amazingly accessible, and their wives were remarkably hospitable as well. Professor Eric Harrison from the History Department arranged that Phyllis Nunn and I shared the scholarship which took us to the Zimmern School of International Studies in Geneva in the summer of 1937 just after we graduated.

That summer was one of the most exciting of my life. At the Zimmern School we were with forty or fifty young people from Britain, France, Germany, Czechoslovakia, Austria, Turkey, Egypt, the Scandinavian countries, Finland and, of course, the United States, for nearly two months. The school was the very personal enterprise of Sir Alfred Zimmern, well known as an historian of classical Greece, and his mercurial French wife. Dedicated to the concept of collective security and to the League of Nations, the Zimmerns were deeply troubled that summer by the perilously uncertain state of European peace, and the prospect of a gravely weakened League. The summer was a stimulating round of argument which put flesh and blood on all one's academic notions.

That winter my sister and her husband were home with us on furlough from India. Their first child was born in Ottawa at Christmas time and I was much involved in family affairs. Not much more than six months after they left us to return to Agra, my father died suddenly and totally unexpectedly of a massive coronary thrombosis. It was a watershed in my life. The pattern was shattered.

In our distress my mother and I retreated to Halifax to the home of my Aunt May and Uncle Jim Falconer at Pine Hill Theological College, where he was a long-time professor. During the thirties through my undergraduate years at Queen's I was under no pressure to get a job, and I had no clear idea where my interest in history and economics, and especially international affairs, would lead me. I can even remember maintaining rather naively that I ought not to take a paid job lest I deprive some man or woman with a family to support of the means to do so. But when my father died it became abundantly clear that I must decide, and quickly, what I was going to do for a living, and how I could set about getting the necessary qualifications. It took me little time to make up my mind to return to university in quest of a doctorate, with the hope of getting a university teaching appointment in due course. International relations was still my chosen focus, and even at that time I had a sneaking hope that I might find a chink through which I might squeeze my way into the Department of External Affairs. Queen's was more than hospitable to me as a graduate student and gave me a generous fellowship and a pleasant job as Warden of Goodwin House, which provided me with free board and lodging.

I had been doing a good deal of work in the area of Canadian-American relations and chose as my MA thesis topic to examine Canadian opinion on American neutrality in the 1914-1918 war. I depended heavily on contemporary newspapers and periodicals which I poured over in the Douglas Library and also in the Public Archives and Parliamentary Library in Ottawa. You could stay all night in the Public Archives if you were prepared to be locked in between 2 and 3 am when the night watchman was off making his rounds of the cellars and the attics. It was an eerie experience. I delivered my thesis at the end of the summer and in due course received my Master's degree.

The history of Canadian-American relations was still a somewhat neglected field in 1940. I decided to pursue it further in my doctoral thesis and hoped to find out what I could of Canadian-American-British economic cooperation in the First World War period.

Winning the Marty Scholarship for the 1940-41 academic year was of course the key to these plans, and my gratitude was, and is, profound. I registered at Radcliffe College in the doctoral program in history. The Radcliffe and Harvard graduate schools were, for all practical purposes, merged. In the first year I was required to carry a full course load with term papers but no major thesis. I seem to remember getting A's across the board, which brought a Master's degree almost automatically. Queen's had been much more demanding!

In the spring of 1941 I applied for, and won, the University Women's Club Travelling Fellowship. I wrote my application while suffering from a humiliating case of German measles, and I have always suspected that a rather high fever possibly sharpened my wits and my pen. Because of this success I refused two interesting job offers: one was a donship at McGill, and the second, a junior position on the staff of the Canadian Institute of International Affairs in Toronto. I wonder where either of them might have led me?

Back again at Harvard I passed the required tests to establish that I had a reading knowledge of French and German, and settled down in a stall in stack 'D' of Widener Library to prepare for the next hurdle, my 'generals.' A panel of experts would examine me, face to face, on the five broad areas of history I had chosen to offer. Stack 'D,' far below ground level, held the Canadian collection. It also held three other Canadians: Arthur Menzies, an Ambassador-to-be, Gerald Graham, a one-time Queen's professor who eventually would settle at King's College, University of London, and finally Eugene Forsey, whom everyone knows. A little hob-nobbing was an acceptable diversion.

Not far into the autumn I received, greatly to my surprise, a note from the History Department telling me that I had been excused my generals and might proceed forthwith to the preparation of my doctoral thesis. This ought to have been splendid news, but I had been running into difficulties. I was beginning to feel less and less happy about my thesis subject. Material was scarce, and I felt sure that access to relevant government documents was becoming impossible with the progress of war. Officials were unlikely to have time for starting up a search for reports of meetings of forgotten joint committees of an earlier war. My supervisor was overworked and not much interested in my subject, which was in a field he claimed no familiarity with. In fact, he more or less indicated that I was on my own.

My mother and I were still based in Halifax and returned there every summer. In Nova Scotia, the war seemed close. Halifax harbour and Bedford Basin were carpeted wall to wall with cargo boats assembling for the perilous trip across the Atlantic in convoy. Black-out curtains were pulled every night and Halifax was overflowing with service men.

The war as seen from Cambridge, Massachusetts, was a very different matter. When my mother and I arrived in the autumn of 1940 I was stunned to find that many Radcliffe students simply took for granted that the British were already beaten and would very soon give up. Having been steeped in the study of Canadian-American relations for the last year at Queen's, I took the situation with a degree of resignation and understanding. Not so my mother. British to the core, she would address me, her unwilling stooge, in ringing tones meant for the public at large, on the iniquities of the Americans. They should be down on their knees thanking God for the English who were fighting their battles for them. This was her theme in restaurants, in the subway, on street corners and in church. Then Pearl Harbour happened and all sides stopped talking.

It was shortly after the Americans came into the war that I began to feel a serious dissatisfaction with my position. I remember my three years of graduate study as a time of pressure such as I had never felt before. I was being financed by generous benefactors to whom I felt a heavy obligation to perform well. This was a marked change of mood from the light-hearted enthusiasm of earlier days, when I was answerable to no one but myself and worked hard for the love of it. The loss of a dearly loved father and my concern for my mother, who never really recovered from the blow and was devastatingly lonely for the remaining twenty years of her life, were a sort of under-tow dragging at my spirits. War was ever present. We realized bleakly that we would not now see my sister and her family, caught in India, until after it was over. I was feeling more and more the need to get home to Canada and make some contribution, however small, to the war effort.

I do not remember how I found out that the Department of External Affairs was looking for women with the required qualifications to work in the Department as Grade IV clerks at the princely salary of $1640 per annum. It was the first time that External had opened the door even a crack to women other than for secretarial/stenographic positions. I applied at once, and sat for the examination.

Time passed and there came a telegram from Hugh Keenleyside: 'Can you do typing and shorthand?' I was sorely tempted to reply 'No, can you?' but, sensing that would certainly spell the end of any hope of a job in External, I settled for 'Little typing and less shorthand.' The next telegram offered me a job in something called 'Central Registry.' Office jargon is not your average graduate student's expertise, and neither I nor my friends had any idea what this meant, but we feared the worst. I decided to go up to Ottawa and find out. I called on George Glazebrook, who was an old acquaintance. He admitted that Central Registry was indeed the filing department, but suggested that it would be a fine opportunity to find out what was happening in the Department. But my Honours BA in History and Economics, my two MA degrees in History, and a further year's work, albeit not a very profitable one, on a doctoral thesis rose up before me, and I said, 'No thank you.' I walked two blocks and got a job in the Wartime Prices and Trade Board. I was paid $1800 a year plus cost of living bonus, which brought my monthly pay cheque to nearly $200. I have never felt wealthier in my life, and the burdens of the last three years floated away. Sometime later External Affairs did offer me another job but by that time I was deeply involved in price controls and did not pursue it.

My boss was Kenneth Taylor, the Secretary, warm, friendly and wise, a former professor at McMaster University. I was one of a group of young people in the crowded central office. We were handed a batch of correspondence each morning, requiring a little or a lot of research and a draft reply for the signature of one or another of top brass types. We also vetted and edited Board Orders. As I circulated around the building seeking information I came on many familiar faces from pre-war Ottawa, Queen's, or Toronto with whom I felt comfortable and at home, and I was happy. I shared a flat with friends who dated back to my Toronto school days, and the people we met at work made up a compatible company.

In the fall of 1942 Phyllis Turner persuaded me to move to a position which had opened up in the Commodity Prices Stabilization Corporation. The CPSC was the subsidy-paying and bulk-purchasing branch of the Wartime Prices and Trade Board. Phyllis had been appointed by my father as an economist to the Tariff Board and had been an indispensable support to him until he died. She was now the Wartime Prices Administrator of Oils and Fats. The President of CPSC was Hector McKinnon, who had succeeded my father at the Tariff Board. He was a dear friend, and for me forever the model of the perfect civil servant. I was to work with Irene Spry, a Cambridge-trained professor of economics from the University of Toronto, whom I had not met, but whose husband, Graham, I had known since I was a teenager. I moved into this friendly milieu and remained there until the whole price control structure was dismantled seven years later, its mission accomplished.

In very general terms, the mandate of CPSC was to provide subsidies, under stringent conditions, to cover uncontrollable cost increases in the production or importation of consumer goods, to enable them to be sold to the public under the price ceiling. In the case of a broad range of off-shore commodities in short supply, CPSC actually purchased goods abroad and distributed them through the normal channels to the domestic market at less than cost. Later I was chief of what was called the Research Division. It was our business to keep track of every type of subsidy scheme and bulk purchasing arrangement and to provide information on demand to the Minister of Finance, Members of Parliament, or whoever required it.

My wartime experience gave me a close up and tremendously interesting view of the nuts and bolts of the Canadian economy. As time went on my responsibilities at CPSC grew and I became part of the executive committee dealing daily with the current batch of subsidy payments. I also was alternate member for Canada on a joint committee on oils and fats, meeting in Washington to discuss needs and availability and to make allocations. A reporter on the *Ottawa Journal* discovered, after a bit of research, that I was the highest paid woman in the Civil Service. I put this down not to any special distinction on my part, but to the fair-mindedness of Hector MacKinnon and his successors who headed up the corporation. I have never, once established in a job, been aware of any discrimination against me because of my sex. Getting into the job was the challenge.

At the end of the war I suppose it might have been expected that I would return to Harvard and tackle a doctoral thesis. Those whose academic progress had been interrupted by the war were given a very generous extension of time in which to do this, but I never seriously considered picking up those torn threads again. I was happy in government service and determined to stick with it. I entered a competition for Department of Finance Officers Grade 3. I was placed on the 'eligible for employment' list, but was never offered a job. The doors of Finance, like those of External Affairs, did not at that time readily open for women.

In the end my choice was between Trade and Commerce and the Tariff Board, both of which were prepared to take me on as an Economist Grade 9. The significance of the number nine now eludes me. Could there possibly have been eight other grades of economists? Since Hector MacKinnon had returned to the Chairman's desk at the Tariff Board after an extended round of trade negotiations, I jumped at the chance to work with him again. My work was to study, report and make recommendations on the structure of the tariffs affecting particular industries. We were a small, cheerful organization. Many of the staff were friends from my father's days.

Outside office walls, too, the wartime stress was easing. My sister and her family came home from India in 1946. My brother-in-law arranged to take his discharge from the Indian Army in Canada. He went back to university and became an Anglican priest. My mother and I revelled in being once more part of a larger family group, and I was captivated for all time by my niece and my two nephews. There was time to develop other interests. A number of us started a local women's branch of the Canadian Institute of International Affairs. I sat on the Marty Scholarship Committee for a number of years, and served on the Queen's University Council for eighteen years. This connection with Queen's meant a great deal to me and I have missed it ever since.

Through this account I have had little to say about friends, not because they are unimportant but because they are so important that I cannot tackle them on the scale they deserve. They must be another story. I must mention, however, two of my dearest friends, Marjorie and Lois Gordon, both of whom had distinguished careers. I lived with each of them at different times during the war. Dr C.W. Gordon was their father, a greatly loved United Church minister, and, under the name of Ralph Connor, author of many novels about Canada. Through Marjorie and Lois I came to know their sister Mary and her husband, Humphrey Carver. During his wartime service in the Canadian Army, Humphrey was on the staff of the Directorate of Personnel Selection and was much in Ottawa. I met their son Peter when he was perhaps seven or eight and on a visit from Toronto with his mother.

Humphrey has told his story in his book *Compassionate Landscape*, which was published in 1975. I will not repeat it. Mary died in January 1948. She was a lovely, vivid person, and I thank God I knew her. Humphrey and Peter moved to Ottawa that summer and Humphrey began a new job with Central Mortgage and Housing Corporation. On November 26, 1951, Humphrey and I were married.

We had agreed that I would retire when I had dealt with the unfinished business on my desk. Today many young women would ask, why? My answer would be that Humphrey and Peter seemed enormously more important than anything else. We did not need two salaries. When we were married I was earning only slightly less than Humphrey. I had had a satisfying and moderately successful career for just short of ten years. I was in no doubt about whether I could operate adequately in a competitive society. I think I was lucky. Women coming into the labour market ten or twelve years later than I had far more trouble in becoming established. They had to face the fact that the men who returned to the universities after the war were a mature and experienced lot with a real advantage over their competitors, male or female.

In 1951 married women were not yet permitted to be permanent civil servants. My contributions to pension were returned to me, effective the day I was married. I finished up a report on the Canadian plastics industry, and also a brief study on the tariff on engineers' and architects' plans. My last task for the Tariff Board was to be locked up with the Press on the day in April when the Budget was brought down, so that I could answer any questions which might arise on aspects of recommended changes in tariffs. Later I was urged to go back to the Tariff Board to deal with a reference on wool and the woollen industry when my daughter Deborah was less than a year old. I knew that I would not be able to change mental gears quickly enough to handle a baby and wool at the same time, and I refused. Perhaps that was due to age. As the next twenty years rolled on I became heavily involved in voluntary work in everything from pre-school education and day care to mental health services for children and meals on wheels for the elderly. I was one of the committee who set up the Central Volunteer Bureau, was for years a member of the Board of the

Social Planning Council, the Budget Committee of the United Way, and President of the Andrew Fleck Child Centre. I was not idle, but I missed the challenge of having to stretch my brain in something which was more in my professional field. It was a pleasure to do a study for the Royal Commission on the Status of Women, on women in political activities in Canada. It was beyond belief satisfying, when my younger daughter was finishing her last year at high school and heading for Trent University, to be appointed a Commissioner of the Canadian Transport Commission where I spent the eight most richly interesting and demanding years of my professional career.

But the things I have been talking about are peripheral to the long, rewarding family years. I have now been married to Hump for thirty-five years, close to half my life. These years form a whole, and do not lend themselves to chronological treatment. Our lives and those of our children are a complex of interweaving relationships which change, get more intricate in pattern, grow thicker or become more attenuated, produce rich colour here, and pastels there.

Let us go back to the barn where this essay began. Here is my family on my seventy-second birthday. The lobster birthday party is taking place as predicted. There are twenty-four of us, six neighbours and eighteen family. The people around the table are what they have been, what they are and what they will be. From the start we have all had a part in each other.

But I have not, in the broadest sense, dealt with Humphrey's question, 'What are we doing here?' The Presbyterian Shorter Catechism comes right to the point with its very first question. 'What is the chief end of man?' it asks, and the answer is, 'Man's chief end is to glorify God and enjoy Him forever.' This unequivocal statement as to what we humans ought to be doing on earth has been running through my mind as I pursued this exercise in self scrutiny. The wording which satisfies me is clearly incompatible with the mind-set of most of my children's generation. But if one can tolerate the use of the concept 'love' as being the basic creative force, rather than using the word 'God,' I think the ancient affirmation might accommodate handily the aspirations and enthusiasms and joys of the young people here.

Change and changing

ELEANOR CLARKE HAY

Looking back, for me, is like being in a museum. Everywhere I see odd items that no longer seem a part of me. They are organized in a variety of showcases. Some are brightly lit and others lie in dim shadows. Some are beautiful and others are ugly or frightening. I ask myself: 'How many of the items in these cases are truly part of my experience, and how many are merely part of my remembrances?' Perhaps if they are sufficiently meaningful to remember, there may be no essential difference between the two.

I was born in April of 1915 in the smelting town of Coniston, Ontario. This was nineteen months after the birth of my twin sisters, and less than three years after my parents had been married.

As long as I can remember, I was sure that I was not a wanted child. Eventually my mother told me of the circumstances of my conception and what a trial my birth had been. It helped to know, but it no longer mattered. I was an infant of the wrong sex, wrongly conceived at the wrong time. I became acceptable and approved by my parents only after I left home.

As a child I imagined that I was adopted. One day I would find my real parents, and would live happily ever after. Meanwhile, I sat on a footstool at the feet of the tall and graceful mother of my best friend. She taught me to memorize poetry and Bible verses. Also, I visited a round old lady who had no children. She hugged me, gave me cookies and taught me to embroider. In the supportive embrace of our town's three-room grade school I passed provincial examinations for eight grades in five years.

My girl friend and I wished that we were boys. We took boys' names. We climbed to the rafters of her house and considered hiding in the empty spaces we could see below. It never occurred to us that had we let ourselves down into those spaces, we might have dropped through the ceiling. We shared secrets at the 'Council Rock' west of town and buried our codes

Eleanor Clarke Hay, 1940

there. She told me that her parents shouted at each other. Mine didn't. Our parents read to us, played classical records on a wind-up phonograph, brought us to concerts held in a skating rink eight miles away, took us canoeing on Sundays. We fished, snared and hunted. We tramped, snowshoed and skated. From the time I was three until I was ten, the family holidayed each year for two weeks by canoe in a different wilderness area of Northern Ontario. We never thought of wearing bathing suits.

My brother was born when I was ten. Everybody rejoiced. He was given my boy's name. I did not mind. My body grew up very early. My sisters considered my breasts very ugly, especially since they did not have any yet.

After grade school, my girl friend was sent to boarding school. My sisters went to live with maiden friends of my mother's. I was kept home. My parents considered me unreliable. They were correct. I had no intention of being reliable. I played hockey with the boys, rode my bicycle miles and miles out of bounds, splashed ink on my new clothes, crept over the tracks to cut willow for whistles and poplar for a spear. As I whittled I imagined myself as Sir Lancelot in white armor.

When I entered Continuation School at the age of twelve, I met a teacher who motivated me to study. Mr Frank Purdy introduced all the students in his two-room school to experimentation. The experiments did not always go as planned. Mother taught me Latin, and Father showed me how to organize and classify information. I began to excel in meeting educational requirements. The personal libraries of the families of managers in town were opened to me. I began to build a herbarium of local plants. Eventually it contained about five hundred named specimens. In the process I became aware of different environmental niches.

With the fall of the Stock Market in 1929, my family lost all its savings except for a small sum that my mother had inherited. She would not use it to cover the latest margin call. The Silences descended on our house. Mond Nickel Company merged with International Nickel. Father's position was eliminated. He was offered a non-managerial position and a tiny house. My parents separated. With the little that she had held on to, Mother bought a house in Kingston.

With his dog for a companion, Father took up residence in a Staff House in Copper Cliff, Ontario. They rationalized that the separation was necessary because my sisters were ready to enter Queen's University. I left Coniston in tears, resolving to be independent as soon as possible. I did not realize what a firm foundation I had been given.

In September of 1930, my twin sisters entered Queen's University, and I registered at Kingston Collegiate Institute. My clothes were wrong. I had never heard of a gymnastic horse, held a basketball, or had to change classes. By Christmas I had acquired a school uniform, learned how to escape being chosen for games that I played poorly, and found a friend. She introduced me to Girl Guides at St George's Cathedral. Each Monday evening I worked on badges. On Sunday I attended evensong. There I revelled in the space, the music – and the presence of my troop leader a few seats away. I became the Tawny Owl of a Brownie Pack at St Paul's Anglican Church, and joined the choir there. I saw death for the first time. One of my brownies died of rheumatic fever. She looked as sweet in death as she had in life.

To ease the financial drain, I marked time until my sisters neared graduation. The extra year in the Collegiate Institute taking business and commercial art courses proved to be one of the most useful of my life.

When I entered Queen's in the fall of 1934, I registered in required courses and electives in which I was sure that I could excel and worked for scholarship standing from day one. Much to my amazement I won three honours: the N.F. Dupuis scholarship in mathematics, the William H. Nicholls scholarship in chemistry, and the Gowan Foundation No. 2 in botany. In philosophy, Dr Gregory Vlastos revolutionized my view of the universe and clarified the concept of freedom. Minnie (Dr Wilhelmina) Gordon, Professor of English, provided a glimpse of what it was like to be a unique woman in a largely masculine environment. Dr MacClement discussed plant taxonomy with me, and urged me to visit the Department of Agriculture in Ottawa. My idea of surveying plant life in the Northwest Territories was not encouraged! Dr Earl, Professor of Biology, demanded that I make choices. I hesitated because it was clear that every choice both opened and closed doors. An opportunity led me to choose among specializing in botany, zoology or chemistry. At the end of my second year I took a part-time job in the Department of Pharmacology. This position, together with prizes and scholarships, gave me a chance for independence. I moved to a room on Earl Street in a house to which my sister Elizabeth had moved a few months before.

In the Department of Pharmacology I helped to prepare and conduct the laboratory experiments required of fourth-year medical students. I organized and indexed drug supplies. Women were not accepted in Medical School, so I became accustomed to being the only woman among many men. I did some routine blood and urine analyses for the Kingston General Hospital, and research analyses for Dr Eldon Boyd's studies on blood lipid levels in health and disease. On my own, I investigated variations in blood iodine levels. For four years, Dr Boyd provided me with freedom, inspiration, opportunities and stability. I left with a Master's Degree in Endocrinology, and a Marty Memorial Scholarship.

To study in England during the war was impossible. At first I planned to go to the University of Minnesota to continue studies on iodine metabolism. The professor with whom I wanted to work moved to Philadelphia and had no room for me.

A meeting of the newly formed Canadian Physiological Society was held at Queen's in the fall of 1940. Dr Boyd urged me to attend. It was there that I met Dr Hans Selye and his students. Dr Selye had just discovered the anesthetic effect of certain steroids in young rats. The pharmaceutical and physiological possibilities excited me. I visited Dr Selye's laboratory in Montreal. We wrote a project proposal which the Marty Memorial Scholarship Committee accepted.

For my doctorate I hoped to explore whether we produce, naturally, agents which mimic morphine. Picrotoxin antagonized the response of the rat to anesthetic steroids and to narcotics. I prepared a film to demonstrate these observations, and showed it in the fall of 1941 at the Annual Meeting of the Canadian Physiological Society. This was all that I was permitted to do on that project. The cost of animals was deemed to be prohibitive.

Students working with Dr Selye were expected to change plans and projects. A promising observation might lead to a host of hypotheses of which only a few could be explored. Then another promising lead took precedence. His decision not to use resources to study the anesthetic effect of steroids in depth was probably a wise one. After twenty-five years of imaginative research in many laboratories, the subject of stress-induced analgesia has still not yielded any medically useful conclusions. Narcotic peptides have been found to be released from the brain into the blood stream under a variety of conditions. Like morphine, they are addictive and induce tolerance. However, we do not know how to elicit a useful analgesic response in a human in a scientifically reliable manner.

I spent five exciting years with Dr Selye at McGill University and the University of Montreal as part of his data-generating team. The project that proved of longest benefit to me was really a side issue. I set up a system by which the results of experiments could be recorded on one standard form. Forms were accessioned serially and sorted according to the procedures used. They were stored centrally in loose-leaf notebooks.

36

For a time, Dr Selye and his students had at their fingertips the results of years of work performed by a variety of students.

In 1943, the month before I was awarded my doctorate, I married Dr Alden W. Hay. He had received his PhD in Physical Chemistry from McGill a year earlier, and was working on explosives with Canadian Industries Limited in Beloeil. I commuted from Beloeil to Montreal until July of 1946.

A woman does not need to lose her independence when she marries. My marriage has liberated me more than it confined me. Chosen physical, mental and emotional commitment is the essence of a free life.

It was not my intent to interrupt my career when our first son was born. Some of my peers managed to continue, but I could not find adequate child care. I am glad that I did not. Rearing children has been an integral part of the fulfillment of my life.

Before our son was a year old, we moved to Madison, New Jersey. My husband became a research specialist in textile design and coloration with Celanese Corporation of America in Summit. I began to manage a three generation house.

I tried to obtain a teaching position at Drew University, a ten-minute walk from our house. The remuneration for part-time work was less than the cost of a baby-sitter!

As a volunteer, I abstracted journal articles sent to me from *Excerpta Medica* and *Biological Abstracts*. When I obtained a contract from Ronald Press to write a popular endocrinology, I joined the library of the New York Academy of Medicine. A Signa Xi-related group called the Summit Association of Scientists provided my husband and me with interesting contacts. We sang classical music with a community choral society. We had two more sons before the first was five.

In the fall of 1953, as my book neared completion, a crisis prevented its reaching publication. The manuscript remains as it was left that day when I was told by the third grade teacher of my eldest son: 'If you don't teach him to write he will never learn.' To me, it was the school's function to teach reading, writing and arithmetic, and my function to teach cultural matters such as self-image, vocabulary, behaviour, oral communication, music, religion, natural science. In these latter areas his progress more than satisfied me.

The crisis became a six-year struggle. We found that he held his breath when he tried to write; and he frequently experienced penile erections which diverted him. I went to his school to see what other children did, and to a psychiatrist to discuss the situation. The psychiatrist gave me a book on the emotional development of children. It contained nothing relevant to a writing difficulty in a child who read at above grade level. To be sure there were emotional consequences of forcing him to write, and permitting him to continue not writing.

I did all the exercises in three writing manuals and chose the style that seemed easiest to learn. Standing at a table, and using finger paints, we made writing a coordinated body exercise, shouting counts for each motion. Counting made him breath. A lesson could end in a frenzied mess.

After five years, he could dictate what he wanted to write. I printed, and he copied the printing. There was and still is a huge gap between what he thinks and what he can put on paper. The last three years of grade school he spent at Admiral Farragut Academy making it on his own. He attended the University of New Brunswick, but withdrew toward the end of his third year. With trade school training and hard work he has become a successful computer technician, programmer and systems analyst, experienced in networking and conversions.

Our other sons were not outstanding students, but both are college graduates.

During the five years of struggle, I studied at Montclair College, Drew University and Fairleigh Dickinson University to become qualified to teach in the State of New Jersey. I threw myself into courses generally considered 'easy bores', read everything proposed, experienced every opportunity offered. In return I learned much about myself. There is more to being a Puritan than having a work ethic and celebrating a traditional Thanksgiving.

Just before reaching certification I experienced secondary shock in association with my last spontaneous abortion. It is truly uncanny how many of the conditions explored in animals in Dr Selye's laboratory I have felt first hand. Without treatment, an animal does not survive hemorrhagic secondary shock. Survival for me was associated with an extracorporeal experience. Within twenty-four hours I knew that I was a different person. A family friend comforted me by saying I was a 'better' person. He could not explain what he meant. I lost what it was that made it possible to make ninety-five to one hundred percent grades, and gained an ability to know from minor clues what people around me are thinking and feeling. My capacity to recall names for people I know remains impaired. To introduce one person to another I need to prepare a hand-held prompt.

Between 1959 and 1964 I taught in the Madison Public School System, first as a substitute and then as a regular teacher. Everywhere I went I

Eleanor Clarke Hay with oldest grandson, Andrew Ralph Hay, July 1986.

carried a copy of the seating chart! As a regular teacher I could not stand the sufferings of the children in my class. We were brought up to think of childhood as carefree. It is not so. A quiet child may be unable to learn the 'nonsense' of the school curriculum because uncontrollable internal feelings, guilts and fears drown the ability to pay attention.

In 1962 I began to abstract under contract a series of journals for CIBA Pharmaceutical Company. This was part of an effort by a group of Swiss and German pharmaceutical firms to build a jointly managed, IBM-card-sortable data base designed to relate chemical structure to biological activity. The data base eventually grew into the Derwent service called RINGDOC. Abstracting led to my being asked to join the Scientific Information Centre of CIBA's Research Department in Summit, New Jersey.

As a Senior Information Scientist I read journals, answered requests for information, attended Biological Research Staff meetings and provided specific staff members with articles relevant to their work. In six months I felt proficient. It took much longer to be sure that my work was profitable. In industry, a scientist is not free to follow his or her interest while on the job. Research in Summit was part of a world-wide program planned primarily in Switzerland. I was permitted to see documents dealing with plans as they influenced investigations in the United States.

In 1966, as Supervisor of Biological Services, I took over an abortive attempt to systematize the reporting of the biological activities of chemical entities being prepared by research chemists in Summit. It was my task to develop forms for input that were acceptable to biologists and chemists, and were compatible with the software provided. The system was updated monthly from 1966 to 1985. It was converted twice: once in 1970 when CIBA and Geigy merged, and a second time in 1985 when individual laboratories acquired the ability to enter and retrieve their own primary data on-line. Twenty years of summary data remain searchable.

Following the merger of CIBA and Geigy, scientists in the two pharmaceutical research organizations needed to create central information files, managed by a Senior Chemical Information Scientist. When this person retired in 1973, the responsibility for the files and their staff was transferred to me. The Document Information System Management (DISM) started in July of 1977 with a staff of two professional scientists, three technical workers, and me as Manager. Microfilmed documents were indexed using a controlled vocabulary. The terms were entered into computer files that could be edited. Corrected files were transferred every night into the data base. By searching the data base on-line, a microimage of the first page of a document could be displayed on a screen, and a copy made. We planned that at the end of five years the pointers for selected documents would be purged on a regular basis. Documents no longer available by on-line searching would be retrieved manually through the use of Computer Output on Microfilm (COM) indexes. This did not prove possible. The data base was converted with new software to storage in updated equipment.

With this job done, I retired in April 1985. During my twenty years with CIBA and CIBA-GEIGY I enjoyed being a key person in a team of pioneers. The friendships that pioneering makes remain.

The award of a Marty Memorial Scholarship, followed by that of a Banting Research Fellowship, was crucial to the route that my life has taken. Without them opportunities for challenging and satisfying work would have been very limited. I enjoy the course that I am running; and I am still running.

Recently a young woman asked me, 'How did you become a liberated woman before it was fashionable?' To those born before 1939 I appear 'liberated'; to those born after 1960 I do not. The militaristic women who organized NOW (National Organization for Women) in the early 1970's did not attract me. I have supported and worked for Civil Rights issues from the time of my student days at Queen's when I went to Indianapolis as a representative of the Student Christian Movement and came face to face with segregation. My black companion from Jamaica and I went in search of places where we could eat together. I also support and work for the adoption of the Equal Rights Amendment to the American Constitution.

I do not consider myself liberated from the constraints commonly experienced by women of my era. Differences between the educational and professional opportunities of girls and boys, men and women, I noted early and continue to see. The driver of a limousine service who is looking for Dr Hay is looking for a man unless he is specifically told to look for a woman. Had registration in the Faculty of Medicine at Queen's University been open to women in 1935 to 1939, I would have become a physician. Women who graduated in Medicine from McGill University experienced the same conflict between professionalism and child-rearing as I. A friend recently commented that women physicians need the services of a wife just as men physicians do, just to free their spare time for self-renewal. My own goals and priorities have limited the level of my contribution to science and society more than the constraints placed by the conventions and prejudices of the community. Fortunately my goals and priorities have changed with the times.

The times have seen two world wars, a great depression, giving women the vote, the expansion of the League of Nations into the United Nations, the breaking of the sound barrier, the smashing of the atom, commercialization of flight, the broadening of civil rights, expansion of the pharmaceutical industry, the legalization of contraception and abortion, the aging of populations in developed countries, transformation of work in America from blue collar to white collar, a rising incidence of homelessness, divorce and one parent households, increased concern for the integrity of our environment on earth and the safety of space. My parents did not have any more stable a life than I; nor did their parents. They had more hope than the children growing up in America today. My children are anticipating change. Economists claim that they and their peers should expect to experience an average of three career paths which require re-education. Although some industries help their employees to shift from one field to another, the help is highly selective. In my experience women do not demand as much as men, and less is expected of them.

In 1984, a young and ambitious college graduate joined my team as a computer operator. For administrative purposes he reported to me. In technical matters he reported to a computer services group. Within a month of his joining CIBA-GEIGY a meeting of managers and directors was scheduled to plan for five years of this employee's career. Never in my experience had such a meeting been held to consider the future of a young and ambitious woman. A woman has to prove her worth before she is considered for opportunities. Courses in assertiveness training are very popular with young women. Graduates, however, need to choose fields where training can pay off. Too many women choose to work in service rather than risk-taking jobs. They remain invisible and poorly paid. I worked in a service-giving department at CIBA-GEIGY. That I was poorly paid did not matter to me at first because so much of what I earned was taxed away. When my husband's field of specialization was closed out and he became 'early retired,' I cared a great deal. I continued to be underpaid until I became a manager. The salary range of my position was not changed for the man who succeeded me.

In my experience the amount of money paid a worker is not related so much to the value of the product or service as to the cost involved in replacing that person. I was paid adequately when it became obvious that I would be expensive to replace. This principle should be used to establish by law the value of the work performed by a man or woman who stays home to manage a household. Such people are expensive to replace. They should be considered self-employed, and should pay social security taxes in the same manner as a lawyer, a physician or a plumber. Such an arrangement would improve the status of homemakers, and perhaps also that of the Social Security system.

Many women complain of sexual harassment. I do not. At the age of eight I crossed paths with a child molester, escaped and seemingly forgot. I told no one because I was in a place where my parents had forbidden me to go. At thirteen I was propositioned by a peer and did not know what he meant. He went away – probably very puzzled. At eighteen I was taken for a walk by a philandering relative, sensed something odd and walked home. At Queen's University I experienced no annoying incidents even as the only woman in a room full of men. I did not tease or flirt. At McGill University I saw and heard about promiscuity on a regular basis. I did not become involved. I had no intention of running the risk of having a child out of wedlock. As a married woman in Madison, New Jersey, I was propositioned three times in forty years: once by a person with whom my husband and I played cards; once by an officer of the church where I sang; and once by a member of a Great Books study group; never in a place of work. The child molester was the only person who had a lasting effect.

As a college student I was aware of being afraid of certain men and at the same time attracted to them. They were all similar physically. Lorne Greene was one of these people. I had a part in a play with him and was so frightened that I could not remember my lines. I withdrew from the Drama Club. Years later when I saw him play the part of an unshaven graying man in a television show I suddenly remembered the molester of my childhood. The fear turned to laughter. How many men had I puzzled with that push-me-pull-me fear?

Change and changing are key words in my life. Once I might have classified them as good, bad or indifferent. Today they have no moral dimensions. Changes are like the tides of the ocean, the rising and setting of the sun, the coming and going of rain. They have short and long-term rhythms. Both are part of what is. Growing up and growing old are part of what is. With gratitude I am enjoying my adventure, change by change.

A Marty scholar's adventures

JOYCE HEMLOW

In 1942 the Aletta Marty Memorial Scholarship carried two major advantages: first, the opportunity and financial security for a year of study and, equally important, the solid foundation or preparation of the Queen's Honours degree, in my case, in English Language and Literature.

'Read,' said Professor James A. Roy, trying not to be too discouraged by the abysmal ignorance of those of us who, coming from country schools, had had little opportunity to read anything beyond our school-books. 'Read Cobbett's *Rural Rides*,' he advised, in an effort to fill in the English background of the Romantic poets he was trying to teach. 'Learn words, learn to read,' said Professor Henry Alexander, 'not only in Modern English but also in Anglo-Saxon and Middle English (Chaucer).' His fascination with words or rather 'usage' was contagious. 'Read carefully,' said George Herbert Clarke, as he spent one whole term on Tennyson's *In Memoriam*. Dr Clarke wrote stately and dignified poems but saw no reason that right choice of words, cadence, rhythm, balance and beauty should be confined to poetry. 'Do you not see the difference?' he asked, after rephrasing some infelicitous sentence (among many such) in my Master's thesis on Thomas Hardy. I could not. Later, however, I could when in professorial shoes myself I posed the same question to honours and graduate students at McGill.

Graduate School at Harvard proved not unlike Queen's in its priorities and, though fearsome, was not, therefore, daunting. Widener was large, much larger than the Douglas Library at Queen's; the floors of stacks were immense, the reading lists longer, much longer than those at Queen's, more searching, opening up far vistas into the literatures of the past. The linguistic requirements included not only Anglo-Saxon and Middle English but also Gothic (or Old Norse) as well as rapid reading knowledges of Latin (or Greek), French, and German (with few exceptions allowed).

With courses completed and language requirements satisfied, there loomed the dreaded 'Harvard Oral', for which the only safe preparation was to have read everything. This occupation of a lifetime or of many lifetimes was cut short by the able, wise, and watchful Dean of Radcliffe, Bernice Brown Cronkite, who with a telephone call to Warren House (Head Quarters of the Department of English at Harvard) set a firm date arbitrarily. To be faced were five examiners, five Harvard Professors in their respective fields of expertise.

We did not know anything about computers in those days, but in such electrifying situations the mind is a wonderfully alert computer, which, at the excitation of question after question can come up like an unfeeling automaton with information laid down (or 'fed in') years and years ago. Useful indeed now was the solid reading of the Queen's Honours Degree and even a packed little *History of Literature* by one J.M.D. Meiklejohn, mercilessly prescribed in Grade XI or XII in Sydney Academy, Nova Scotia. 'You will never in your life know as much as you did today,' remarked the much feared but really kind Francis Peabody Magoun, as we crossed the Harvard Yard when all was over.

Money was running out. The Marty Travelling Scholarship, supplemented at Radcliffe by a Burshey Scholarship and, for a second year, a Fellowship kindly granted by the Canadian Federation of University Women, had supported work thus far. Assistantships, first to Douglas Bush, eminent seventeenth-century authority, and then to George Sherburn, editor of Pope, were invaluable not only for the stipends they provided but also for experience in the detailed marking of tests and examinations. Papers that I had failed they would re-read to see that no injustice was done. Still to be written, however, was the doctoral dissertation. I needed a subject, short and easy, one that could be completed in a short time.

'How would it be,' I asked Mr Sherburn, as we crossed Harvard Yard to one of his undergraduate classes, 'how would it be if I wrote my thesis on Fanny Burney?' 'Fanny Burney and the Comic Spirit,' I added. I expected him to spurn such a light and attractive subject but, instead, he looked very thoughtful. 'Well, yes,' he replied, 'and if the Burney Manuscripts appear, you could be their editor.' I scarcely knew in those days what a manuscript was and cheerfully I set to work on the Comic Spirit, though what I saw was not so comic after all. Investigations into the nature of comedy, that is, variations from the norm, led into investigations of the norms of conduct and behaviour. Fanny Burney, novelist, journalist, and playwright, planned three of her novels on variants

Joyce Hemlow, PhD LLD FRSC.

from the ethical and social norms (or accepted forms of conduct in her day). These 'errors', though often comic, usually proved very costly to her youthful heroines Evelina, Cecilia, and Camilla. For the eighteenth-century young lady there were guides widely available in elegantly bound little books, manuals of ethics and behaviour like Mrs Chapone's *Letters on the Improvement of the Mind* or Dr Gregory's *A Father's Legacy to His Daughters*, or in volumes of sermons like those of James Fordyce, who unabashedly taught the young lady how to attain the chief end of her being in marriage as well as heaven in the hereafter. No good could be expected of the young lady who yawned over Fordyce or cut pages from his *Sermons* for curl papers. One could characterize her, as both Sheridan and Jane Austen knew, from her attitude to the Conduct or Courtesy Books. Motherless little girls like Fanny Burney studied these guides very attentively, and through them a latter-day student could get to know something of the formation of the eighteenth-century mind. No sooner was my thesis 'Fanny Burney and the Courtesy Books' completed than, as the informed and sagacious George Sherburn envisaged, the Burney Papers, lost to scholars for a century and believed burned, came tumbling forth from attics, trunks, repositories, and private libraries into the public domain. Providentially, a huge segment of them had crossed the Atlantic and come to rest permanently in the Berg Collection of the New York Public Library.

How this came about will be explained later on. Suffice it to say here that a rich archive of family papers, acquired by a bookseller in High Holborn for a few hundred pounds, was purchased allegedly for $120,000 by the American industrialist Owen D. Young. Mr Young had the bundles of manuscripts sorted and encased in handsome custom-made fire-proofed boxes of blue morocco leather. One elegant box contained the fragile but priceless manuscript of Fanny Burney's first novel *Evelina* (1778). Another enclosed her dramatic works: four comedies, of which little was known, and four tragedies composed in her last years at Court. The boxes reposed, a fine acquisition and an ornament, in a sumptuous library, or so one may imagine, until in 1941 Mr Young offered them (partly by sale and partly by gift) to the Berg Collection of the New York Public Library. For safety during the Second World War, the Papers were deposited under some mountain, I believe, but around 1947 they were made available to qualified readers. This was an invaluable archive of eighteenth-century manuscripts which no professional scholar had had access to or the opportunity to examine. But what was their nature and who were the Burneys?

The Burney Manuscripts consist, first, of the correspondence and the extant 'Memoirs' of the versatile and social Charles Burney (1726-1814),

MusDoc, music teacher and Historian of Music. In the heyday of his professional career he was abroad all day teaching young ladies how to play the harpsichord, but not, of course, too well, as no young lady should appear a professional. He seemed to know most of the notables of the age, Garrick, Dr Johnson himself, Burke, Sir Joshua Reynolds, the Earl of Sandwich (notorious First Lord of the Admiralty), Canning, Erskine, and that most comical and lovable of all eighteenth-century men, Aristotelian Twining. He had, as it would have been put then, 'great powers of pleasing' and great powers of mind too. His *History of Music* brought him literary fame in his day; and his letters when published will make one of the liveliest collections yet printed of eighteenth-century correspondence.

The Burney papers include as well the correspondence and the writings of Dr Burney's remarkable family. There were six surviving children by his first marriage and two by his second, and most of them took to scribbling as ducks to water. The second surviving daughter, Fanny (1752-1840), novelist, journalist, and dramatist, won fame very early with the secret writing and anonymous publication of *Evelina, or, a Young Lady's Entrance into the World* (1778). A second novel *Cecilia, or Memoirs of an Heiress* (1782) gained the attention and the approval of the Court and led in 1786 to her appointment as Keeper of the Robes to Queen Charlotte. Free in 1791, she could scarcely have dreamed that dire events in France were soon to impinge on her life.

Landing on English shores in the 1790's were French *émigrés* by the hundreds seeking refuge from revolutionary horrors and the guillotine. Among a group of *émigrés* settled in Juniper Hall near Mickleham in Surrey was the impoverished Alexandre-Jean-Baptiste Piochard d'Arblay, the details of whose courtship of Fanny Burney she made the subject of one of her most delightful journals. Objections to the marriage there were, principally for practical reasons on the part of Dr Burney, but the marriage took place notwithstanding in the parish church at Mickleham on 28 July 1793. Supported by Fanny's pension, granted and continued by Queen Charlotte, and by the proceeds of a third novel *Camilla: or, a Picture of Youth* (1796), the couple lived quietly in Great Bookham, Surrey, where in 1794 their son Alexander was born. In 1797 they moved into Camilla Cottage, West Humble, newly constructed from money realized from hundreds of subscriptions to the novel *Camilla*. This was a happy period, a Surrey idyll, soon to be disrupted by changing events in France.

With the Peace of Amiens (1802) d'Arblay returned to Paris to claim compensation for his confiscated lands and to establish himself in his military profession. A commission offered by the First Consul Napoleon was promptly lost by his refusal ever to take up arms against England. Forced into civil life, he eventually found employment as a *rédacteur* in the Ministry of the Interior. In the spring of 1802 Fanny and her son Alexander, then aged seven, joined him in Paris. Ten years in exile there, as war again broke out between France and England, she found subjects for her pen in new surroundings, French institutions, manners, customs, and the events of the Napoleonic era. A journal of interest to surgeons today is her account of the mastectomy she endured, without anaesthetics, at the hands of Napoleon's famous army surgeon Baron Larrey. In 1815 at the return of Napoleon from Elba she was to participate in a fearful flight to Brussels and there later to hear reverberations from the cannon at Waterloo and witness the ghastly aftermath of battle.

Many of her longest, most intimate and confidential journals (including the Streatham Journals and the Court Journals) Fanny wrote for her favourite sister, Susanna Elizabeth Phillips (1755-1800), who composed thick packets of confidential matter in return. Such communication between the Burneys was fostered by absences from home. In the good eighteenth-century style of life there was a great deal of visiting – visits that tended to last from one to three months. A little Burney with weak lungs could be sent to King's Lynn, Norfolk, for change of air; or to an uncle's house in Worcester, where resided a large family of cousins; or to a boarding house in Chessington with the beloved Samuel or 'Daddy' Crisp. There would still be a Burney or two left in London; and London, after all, was where the most interesting things could happen. The Burney left at home would be charged to keep *most exact journals* or accounts of all that happened there in exchange for journals describing in the most lively, entertaining and realistic way all that had taken place abroad. This was a traffic carefully hidden from the elders. It was free, spontaneous, and confidential. The purpose was not only to inform but also to amuse and entertain. Amusing still, they serve also as first-hand historical pieces or vignettes cited and used to this day.

In the long years of Fanny's widowhood in London (1818-1840) her youngest sister, Charlotte Broome (1761-1838), was her greatest solace and comfort. As old ladies they could confide in perfect trust in each other, discuss legal matters, the making of wills, for instance, and share prescriptions for diet and medicine. 'Eat *something*, however light and trifling,' Fanny begged, 'an egg beat up with warm water and sugar – a Jelly. ...' Charlotte could understand her sister's concern: 'Having lost so many darlings, only renders us still more distracted at the thoughts of fresh bereavements.'

In the 1830's as survivors of a large and famous family they felt responsible for the preservation of family papers and anxiously they consulted on the disposition of accumulated hoards of manuscripts. 'Burn them, Mama,' had been son Alex's advice to Fanny while he lived. Charlotte dared not advise her 'to Burn' but 'pondering – pondering – pondering – Ruminating', she attained a view almost prophetic with respect to the Burney-d'Arblay manuscripts:

So celebrated as your name is, it strikes me, that, *sooner*, or *later* ... they may fall in the hands of some one who will send all to a Bookseller to publish – therefore, if there are any MSS that you *really* wish *never* to be published – the *only safe* way will be to Burn those *particular* MSS – tho' it would be a million of pities So to do – but, it is highly needful for you to do *something* to make your dear torn mind Easy ...

Fanny immersed herself in this editorial work for nearly twenty years, burning papers that she thought would bring discredit to the Burney family or harm others. Often she would obliterate sentences, paragraphs, sometimes whole pages with a series of heavily-linked overlapping o's – drastic measures that presented real challenges to her twentieth-century editors.

Suddenly in the 1940's, as I have explained, an immense segment of these edited papers emerged in the Berg Collection of the New York Public Library, where they were made available to qualified readers. By virtue of my Radcliffe-Harvard degree and my dissertation on Fanny Burney, I was a qualified reader. And this takes me back to my own story.

By this time, happily, I was at McGill University, where research is encouraged to the limits of all available means, and the Dean of Graduate Studies and Research, the late David L. Thomson, realizing the potential of the Burney archives even more clearly than I did myself, allowed me $800, a large sum in those days, for a summer of three or four months in New York to read the Burney manuscripts. At that time permission even to read the papers was considered a great privilege. And it was. Nothing I had ever read, not *War and Peace*, not *The Forsythe Saga*, nothing fictional had interested me as much as the characters, the situations, and the unsolved mysteries drifting through those family papers. One member of the family would write to another with mysterious allusions to a third; the younger generations would comment on their aunts and uncles, great aunts and uncles, divulging secrets carefully kept for years. Skeletons rattled in closets, but the whole story was not there. The supplement or the conjugate part of the archive, I could see, was still in England.

With the help in 1951 of a John Simon Guggenheim Memorial Fellowship I got to England. Following leads in the Burney Scrapbooks in the Berg Collection, genealogical tables and such, I wrote to Burney descendants, and among them, a Miss Ann Julia Wauchope, who lived at Howton, Bushey Heath. I told her about my interest in the Burney family and about the Burney letters I had read in New York. To my astonishment she sent me by registered mail a thick packet of valuable autograph letters with an invitation to tea. On my arrival at Howton I met the owner. She was then in her mid-eighties, but very sprightly and active, with a short thick bob of white hair. Daughter of a clergyman, she seemed to be companion to a wealthy relative, a cousin, who lived in a mansion-like house set in a large garden, which before the war had taken two full-time gardeners to tend. The cousin was dreadfully afflicted with arthritis, moving to the tea-table by a contrivance of canes, straps, and braces, but graciously, notwithstanding a keenly appraising eye for the stranger newly arrived from Canada. I can see the large formal table yet, with its linen, gleaming silver, fine china, flowers, and outside the windows birds singing in the garden. Upstairs in a kind of bedroom *cum* study Miss Wauchope had set forth another kind of table, a library table covered with priceless manuscripts, long and valuable letters, probably crucial, I thought, in the establishment of the Burney story. I asked if it would be possible to stay at the village inn perhaps, come in, read, and take notes. To my surprise she said, 'Ah no, no need', I could take the papers back to London, if I wished. I could hardly credit such trustfulness but said I would bring them back in a week and so did and found the table spread with twice as many. And on the third week, with three times as many, and on the fourth week I went to Bushey Heath with a deep hatbox as the only practicable container for the manuscripts that kept appearing. I began to wonder about the source of this largesse and to look around discreetly for the cornucopia. Finally it was allowed to appear – for we had plumbed its depths – a great black chest pushed under the typically high eighteenth-century bed – the kind old ladies were always falling out of or falling from stools climbing into. Beside it was another trunk of papers, worth in all a fortune. *She it was* who, to relieve debts incurred by her brother, had sold the larger segment of the archive to a London bookseller for 300 pounds. This was the large archive that the Holborn bookseller had sold to the American industrialist Owen D. Young for allegedly $120,000 –

papers that, according to Dr John D. Gordan, Curator of the Berg Collection, could not in the market of the 1950's be bought piece by piece for a million dollars. Until I appeared she had not known what had become of the manuscripts that the London bookseller and his son had taken from her father's vicarage in Southampton some thirty years before. She had not expected perhaps that the papers would leave England. And now at the age when one must think of the disposal of effects she had decisions to make about the residual part of the archive still in her possession. She remembered that her father had wished it to go to the British Museum. She too wished the papers to go to the British Museum where they could be read, she said, by everyone. From the very first I tried to let her know what even one of the long letters would bring on the market, but on the subject of money she seemed deaf. She knew that at the close of the war the British Museum could pay little if anything, but more important to her was a location where the papers could be made available to all. Yet such was her lady-like diffidence and reserve that she could not summon the courage and assurance to approach the Keepers. Having no such disadvantages, I made the offer: 'Would you like me to speak to them?' 'Oh, would you?' she responded gratefully, and the Keepers lost no time, I can tell you, in setting out for Bushey Heath.

'Get microfilms,' the Johnsonian scholar, the late James L. Clifford, advised me, 'get microfilms of everything.' On my next visit at Howton I explained to Miss Wauchope what microfilms were and how they would enable us to read and study the papers at McGill University, and readily she approved the request on her generous principle, availability to all. Accordingly friends of mine went by car to Bushey Heath, loaded the boot and the backseats with priceless papers and took them to the Senate House of London University to be microfilmed. After the microfilming they went to the British Museum, where they were catalogued and mounted in thirty large volumes entitled *The Barrett Collection of Burney Papers* (Egerton 3690-3708).

The fresh, living, pulsing material from the original manuscripts, the information they afforded, new to the English themselves, and to the devotees of Fanny, and to biographers of Dr Burney, and to everybody, indeed, accounted for the success of my biography *The History of Fanny Burney* (1958), handsomely produced and generously promoted by the Clarendon Press, Oxford. It rated the coveted centre-page review in *The Times* (Thursday, 27 February) and perceptive reviews in the *Sunday Times*, the *Illustrated London News*, and many other publications. No American scholar, George Sherburn remarked, had ever received such a press in

England. The book was awarded the James Tait Black Memorial Book Prize for the best biography published in England in 1958 and later, a very great honour, a British Academy award, the Rose Mary Crawshaw Prize (1960). In Canada it won the Governor General's award for academic non-fiction and it must have contributed to the recognition generously accorded the author when she was made an Honorary Doctor of Laws (Queen's, 1967).

The biography, drawing attention to the value and interest of the untapped Burney material, was an introduction to an even more onerous and exciting enterprise, the editing of the papers in the effort to make them available in print.

There is no space here to describe the organization of the Burney Project at McGill University, which, if not the first, was among the first of the group-projects in the Humanities in Canada. Nor is there space to mention the hundreds of persons first and last who contributed to the editorial effort, rising to challenges extraordinary as in the deciphering and the restoration of manuscripts obliterated, mutilated, and emended by Madame d'Arblay herself and by her first editor, Charlotte Barrett. A second challenge was the location and the cataloguing of the original material scattered far and wide by the vicissitudes of the market, time and chance. There were thousands of letters not only in the Berg and Barrett Collections, already mentioned, but also in the Osborn Collection at Yale, the Comyn Family Collection (England), and, as it would prove, in 125 or more caches, large or small, on both sides of the Atlantic, some 10,000 items in all. This was an exacting search, sustained, however, by hope and curiosity. Who knew what information there might be in a new letter, what key to a mystery?

A third challenge, necessitating many summers of genealogical research in England and in France, was the identification of the persons of all ranks of society emerging in the text, from obscure labourers in the field to the King on the throne; from milliners, mantua-makers, governesses, and beggar-women in the street to Queen Charlotte herself. In such detective work, leading to nooks and crannies all over London, to parishes in the beautiful English countryside, to King's Lynn, Dublin, Bath, Windsor, and Mickleham, to County Record Offices in many a county town, to churches, cathedrals, and graveyards everywhere, and finally to the Public Records Office (for wills), – in such searches time passes very quickly. Almost thirty years, in fact, went by, in which time *The Journals and Letters of Fanny Burney (Madame d'Arblay), 1791-1840*, appeared in twelve handsome volumes (Oxford, at the Clarendon Press, 1972-84). The edition was hailed by C.P. Snow as 'one of the triumphs of modern scholarship' and approved by Malcolm Muggeridge as 'meticulously edited and enthralling to read'.

In this international effort to which many persons and institutions have indispensably contributed, it is not difficult to include among many felicitous and seminal circumstances an Aletta Marty Travelling Scholarship that took a Queen's student to Harvard, there to meet, as it evolved, one of the greatest and the wisest of all eighteenth-century scholars, George Sherburn, and this at a time when hoards of important eighteenth-century manuscripts, lost to scholars for a century, were about to break into the public domain.

Dilemmas of a part-time professor

KATHLEEN BUTCHER WHITEHEAD

These are some random thoughts about the career of one woman born in 1920 and who retired from university teaching in 1985. Sometimes things seemed to go along in a well-worn groove but there were also some sharp changes in direction. I think there are some fundamental differences in the pattern of life for many women coming through now but I am only recording a little of my own life.

I come from Western Ontario. My family background is old line English-Canadian – not Family Compact but backwoods. I am approximately three-quarters English and one-quarter Scottish with a bit of Irish. All of my grandparents were born in Ontario but I have cousins spread through the western provinces and in California. One branch of my family came to Niagara with the Loyalists.

My parents were both raised on farms. My father was principal of a small high school and my mother had taught school before her marriage. I have one brother who is four years younger than I. My father had started to teach in a one-room country school and managed by extramural work, summer school and finally a couple of years in residence at Queen's, to receive an Honours BA in mathematics when he was 30. Looking back, I realized that his struggle to get an education had profoundly affected our family life. He was absolutely determined that both his children should go to college. We were never pushed at all. It was just assumed that we would go when the time came. The idea that the girl should get less than the boy was never considered.

My father and mother taught mathematics so that the fact that mathematics was my best subject surprised no one. Now when people are more sensitive about influences on learning and worry about girls being discouraged from taking mathematics, I realize that I never had that experience.

Kathleen Butcher Whitehead, 1980.

When it came time to go to college there were really only three possibilities: Western, Toronto, and Queen's. I chose Queen's because it represented the biggest break from home. My father, being a Queen's graduate, never argued the point. He did insist that I take the scholarship examinations in mathematics, physics, and chemistry. He knew that I had been coasting along and that the problem paper in mathematics would be a challenge. I worked at the old papers. I use the word, 'at' intentionally. On any exam the number of problems I succeeded in doing was not large. Even though my father taught mathematics he couldn't really do the problems either.

I got the scholarship in mathematics. My father had told me that he would give me $1000, but that above that sum I would have to repay him so that my brother could also go to college. High school principals' salaries were not munificent then. With my original scholarship and other prizes I graduated having spent very little more than the $1000. I was free to do what I wanted. My father had always thought that I would teach high school, but I was attracted to working for an insurance company. I had already spent one summer working for the Canada Life.

Then I got a call to go and see Miss Royce. As a freshman I had received a real dressing down from her for failing the Christmas exam in English. She asked if I were interested in going to graduate school. The idea had simply never occurred to me. Going on in mathematics was not the normal thing it became later. She said that the Mathematics Department thought I should consider the possibility. I was completely taken aback, said that I was definitely not interested, and went off. However, she had planted the thought in my mind. That conversation probably represented the first real turning point in my life. Now I had to find out how to go on.

The money problem was perfectly simple – I had none. While I was not in debt, it was now my brother's turn for the family finances. Queen's had a fellowship for a year to get a Master of Arts degree but Professor Halperin, with whom I was already taking a graduate course for fun, insisted I should go immediately to the United States and meet new people. I applied to a few places. Smith College offered me a fellowship which covered room, board and tuition. With that and a travelling fellowship from Queen's I was set for a year.

By the next year I had an MA and was eligible for the Marty. On winning, I chose the University of Michigan in Ann Arbor. These were the war years so I expect it was much easier for a woman to get a fellowship in mathematics. Part way through the year I was told that, since I had a fellowship, I was entitled to a desk in an office for graduate students. They had apparently been unsure about putting a woman in with the men. Once I had a desk, all the other women got desks as available.

It was a good time to be at Michigan. Despite the war there were still enough graduate students to form a group for coffee drinking; one probably learns as much there as in class. Also, while some members of the faculty were away at times, there were plenty of classes and seminars. At the same time it was not the mammoth place it became after the war. With further fellowships from the Canadian Federation of University Women and the University of Michigan, I managed financially. In my last summer my father gave me a few hundred dollars which really went to get me started on a job. Queen's hadn't been what one would call a dressy place and four years of buying almost nothing had left some holes in my wardrobe.

I had always intended to return to Canada when I finished graduate school and, in the summer of 1945, I attended the first Canadian Congress of Mathematicians which was held in Montreal. I expected to receive a PhD in another year. The war was just coming to an end and the men would be returning. I was told flatly that the possibilities in Canada for a woman in mathematics were very poor and that I had better try the American women's colleges. After the war, when the veterans returned, many things changed. New universities were founded in Canada and there would be many more positions available. But that was all in the future.

At that time women, in general, taught in women's colleges. The process of getting a job was really very simple. The head of the department at Michigan gave me the names of two or three colleges, all women's colleges, which needed an instructor. I got an offer from Wellesley College and collected all the documents necessary to get an immigration visa so that I could work in the United States.

My last summer in Ann Arbor, when I was typing my thesis, I met a young mathematician from Princeton who was teaching in the summer school. When I went east to Wellesley in the fall, I was already considering marriage when my contract was up.

I enjoyed the teaching very much. The older people at Wellesley encouraged me to set aside time for research but I'm afraid that twelve hours of classes a week plus a lot of train trips to Princeton filled my time. Of the five members of the department, two others were young and we usually went to Harvard Colloquium every week; but that was about it. I never did attempt research. I still feel apologetic about that. I let the side down. I believe that I was probably always a good learner but with no gifts of originality. Now I have known a lot of good mathematicians, women as well as men, including married women with children (which I never had). The really creative ones will do research no matter what. I never had that kind of drive! However, I believe that I became a good teacher.

During the year at Wellesley, my husband-to-be accepted a job at Brown University. When I inquired about a job there, I was told that there was a nepotism rule but that I could get a job with the applied math group doing what was then called computing, which meant essentially using a calculator. I had a colleague at Wellesley whose husband had also accepted a job at Brown. After some discussion, it developed that the nepotism rule existed only in the mind of the President. It was quietly forgotten and both she and I were hired to be instructors full time.

We taught a course with an older member of the department who clearly did not think much of the idea of hiring wives. He read us a lecture about not leaving him to do all the work. We were both furious. The two of us shared, with a woman graduate student, a large office which had once been a classroom. The course was almost completely composed of veterans and we took turns running help sessions almost every afternoon, for his students as well as our own. That class gave me a Christmas present. It was the only time that happened to me but I had worked very hard and, being slightly older students, they realized it.

After two years at Brown my husband was offered a job at MIT. We moved to Boston in 1949. From then on I held various part-time jobs including six very interesting years at Brandeis. In 1959, I took a part-time job at Tufts. I really only wanted to teach six hours per week but I agreed to teach nine since they were very short-handed. I liked the people; they said that they liked my work.

There were several other part-time and temporary people in the department, mostly people who had almost completed a PhD from one of the other Boston universities and were earning a little money while they finished. That year I was the only part-time married woman with a PhD and teaching experience on the staff, though there had been several in the past. I had the status of a lecturer, which is a good catch-all rank, and, like all the other part-time people, was paid by the course. But unlike most of the others I had no commitments to another university. I really wanted to be considered a regular member of the department who, while teaching less, would do my share of other department chores, run courses, and make out exams.

That was also the time when inflation began to hit and it was announced that 'everybody' would get approximately an 8% raise. I soon discovered that everybody did not include me. I was upset enough to complain to the acting head of the department. He said that, as far as he knew, part-time people had never got a raise but he would ask. A friend who taught part-time at another local university told me that she had talked them into making her a part-time assistant professor so I broached that idea also. I got my raise and, in another year, the rank too. Of course I was only working half-time and the percentage raises left me still very badly paid, but at least I got them. Fortunately my salary was the cream on our income and did not pay for the meat and potatoes. We always considered that it was for frills and not rent.

At Tufts approximately 70% of any class took calculus at some time in their four years. We did not have many majors but, due to the existence of the engineering school, there was a lot of elementary teaching to do. As time went on the level of research in the department was increased and the teaching load went down, first to nine hours per week and then six. The size of the classes went up. I was always given very desirable hours to teach and I had a good reputation so I got big classes. I was still teaching six hours but the work was much harder. I guess about the time the full load was six hours, someone realized that '½ of 6 = 6' was rather odd arithmetic and my contract was changed to part-time instead of half-time. However all seemed fine. I had no tenure but I was a responsible member of the department and was treated as such. I thought they had a good deal. If times changed they could easily not rehire me, and in the meantime they had a very experienced teacher for a very small price.

In the spring of 1973 I took a term of unpaid leave to go to London since my husband had a sabbatical. I, of course, did not qualify for a sabbatical. Over the years my husband had taken fewer leaves than he was entitled to since it was difficult for me to get off. I had to give up a job hoping to get it back. This time I believed I actually had a leave. I certainly was surprised when I got a letter from a colleague telling me that the Dean had decided I must be fired. The head of the department was so mad that he could not bring himself even to write to me. I understand that the various members of the department had gone up personally to complain but the Dean was adamant. When I returned in July, I had waiting for me a one-line letter saying that the next year would be my last. There was also a copy of the letter that the head of the department had written resigning as head. I saw three different officials who gave me three different sets of reasons for the decision. None of them made much sense and in some cases they were contradictory. The only thing they agreed on was that my teaching was fine. In the long run I decided that they were afraid that people like me might start demanding part-time tenure and they were clearing the decks of us all before it happened. I had not even hinted at this idea and frankly I would have considered such a request on my part to be unethical. I had been there fourteen years untenured and to try to get in the back door, so to speak, would not have been right.

Things in the department were now very complicated. The head, whose term had had one more year to run, had resigned; his already designated successor had agreed to take over a year early but only if my situation were satisfactorily resolved; and all the members of the senior administration were on holiday in August. Right after Labor Day, when school was about to start and everybody was very busy, the Math Department was without direction. At this time someone outside the department came up with the idea that they should make me Administrator of the calculus program and reduce my teaching load to one course. With less than a week to go before classes started this was decided in principle and we all went back to work.

When I say it was decided in principle that is what I mean. It was clear that the department needed some extra help and not just another secretary. The previous head had managed by working every night till eight o'clock. The new head had insisted that more help must be forthcoming but nothing had been worked out. I had never had anything to do with the Administration at the operating level. That first term was a nightmare. I seemed no sooner to get one thing done than something else urgent turned up which had to be done immediately!

The two things which the Administration insisted on were that I should not teach more than one course and that I could not be an Assistant Professor. They invented a new rank of Senior Lecturer just for me. I never did see any sense in this last condition and it always rankled. When I retired in 1985 my department, without my knowledge, went to a great deal of trouble to get me appointed Assistant Professor Emerita. I don't know how that was managed but I appreciated it very much.

Thus for twelve years I taught one course and was unofficially the assistant head of the department. I never had anything to do with the budget or the hiring of full-time members of the department. I appeared on the budget as half-time administrator and one-quarter-time teacher. The sum had to come to less than one. How my salary was split I do not know. I handled all the scheduling of classes, tests and exams. I also handled all the usual student complaints and, since I got complete backing from my superiors, if I said 'no' it meant 'no.'

Kathleen B. Whitehead, retirement party, 1985.

I also did a great deal of student advising, especially during freshman orientation in the fall. I found this contact very enjoyable; I often had ten students in my office at once and a big line outside. It meant long hours for a few days but I felt it was worthwhile.

Many of the other big departments eventually had administrative assistants who did many of the same things that I did but, due to the way my job was 'created,' I think only the Math Department had a faculty member in this post. It was a great advantage to actually know what the courses were about and to have standing in the department. Students behave quite differently under these circumstances!

When I retired last year Tufts looked for and found a replacement for me. She is also a mathematician. Her field is history of mathematics, a difficult field in which to get a job. She has a full-time job with a list of duties. I prepared the list by trying to write down all the things I did. Nobody else really knew exactly what they were.

I always liked to think of myself as a teacher first who happened to do other things. I have always enjoyed teaching very much. I've probably taught more calculus than most mathematicians and I found it exciting. There were always new ways to present things. I will miss that.

From Paris to Péribonka

AUDREY FREEMAN CAMPBELL

There's a divinity that shapes our ends,
Rough-hew them how we will. SHAKESPEARE, *Hamlet*

'AWARDED MARTY SCHOLARSHIP THOUSAND DOLLARS CONGRATULA-
TIONS – SEDGEWICK.'
So read the telegram dated March 13, 1948, and delivered to me at the
Collège Franco-Britannique of the Cité Universitaire in Paris. It was like
manna from heaven. I had been studying at the Sorbonne since November
1946, struggling along on a French Government scholarship which was
not enough to cover my living expenses. I had been obliged to supplement
it by translating French brochures into English for a travel agency and by
teaching English conversation in a suburban school. Winning the Marty
meant that I could devote all my time to my studies.

Imagine my amazement when, on April 10, I received a letter from the
Royal Society of Canada, informing me that I had also been granted one
of its Research Fellowships, valued at $1,500! Since no student could hold
two awards simultaneously, I accepted the more valuable one and withdrew
from the Marty, of which I retained only the honour.

This Royal Society Fellowship was granted to me in order that I might
complete, for a Doctorat d'Université de Paris, a thesis entitled 'Le Canada
vu par les romanciers français depuis Louis Hémon.' What a nightmare it
had been to arrive at that subject! I had hoped to expand for a doctorate
my MA thesis on women in French-Canadian literature, but found too
little material on the topic available in Paris. Since I was still interested in
a Canadian subject, Professor Jean-Marie Carré, of the Institut de
Littératures modernes comparées, suggested that I study French novelists
who had written on Canada. I was already familiar with some of these
writers, and my knowledge of French-Canadian literature provided
excellent background.

As I worked on Louis Hémon, who was to be my starting-point, my interest in him and his *Maria Chapdelaine* began to grow. Today, as then, no other book about Canada is so well known beyond our borders. At the Grasset publishing house, where I went in 1948 to read press clippings on the novelist, I learned that Hémon's sister and daughter were living in Paris. In answer to my letter (like many Parisians, they had no telephone), I received an invitation to tea in their apartment, rue du Général-Niox, near the Porte de Saint-Cloud and the Bois de Boulogne. There I met Louis Hémon's sister, Marie, aged seventy-one, and his daughter, Lydia Kathleen, known to family and friends as Kitty (pronounced Kee-tee). Born in London in 1909, she had been brought to Paris early in 1914, after her father was killed by a train in northern Ontario, to be raised in France by his mother and sister. Little was known at that time about Kitty's mother, Lydia O'Kelly, and the skeletons in the family closet were carefully guarded by Mademoiselle Marie Hémon. I returned several times to their apartment to read Louis Hémon's letters, still unpublished, and other material related to *Maria Chapdelaine*.

In the fall of 1949, after three years at the Cité Universitaire, I decided to look for a French family with whom to live until I finished my doctorate. I wrote to the Hémons for suggestions, and Kitty arranged to meet me in the Luxembourg Gardens. Isaac Newton was hit on the head by an apple; we were hit by a couple of chestnuts (I still have mine). Kitty leaped up from the bench and addressed a playful reproach to one of the chestnuts: 'Tu veux nous avoir, toi!' ('So you're out to get us!') In a flash, the incident revealed a rich and whimsical personality completely suppressed in the presence of her aunt. Much is said about love at first sight. Is there not also friendship at first sight? Certainly, Kitty and I experienced it that day, and we are still close friends. The chestnut had not stunned me, but Kitty's proposal did: 'Would you like to come and live with us?' Impulsively, I accepted, and the direction of my life changed. I moved into their apartment in October 1949 and lived there until early July 1951.

It soon became clear to me that this was a heaven-sent opportunity to devote my entire thesis to Louis Hémon. Monsieur Carré was amazed by the unexpected turn of events and encouraged me in my new plan. My subject became 'Le Canada de Louis Hémon et sa destinée littéraire.'

My daily conversations with Kitty and her aunt, who spoke frequently of 'mon père' and 'mon frère Louis,' provided me with many new details and anecdotes about him. I came to know his family background and the intellectual environment which had molded his childhood and youth. In

Audrey Freeman Campbell. A student in Paris, 1950.

the Hémon home, I met people who had known him and critics who had written about his work. I had at hand all the important editions of his books, as well as many articles and studies about him. I knew about the business dealings of Mesdemoiselles Hémon with the Grasset publishing house and helped to persuade them to release his last important unpublished work, *Monsieur Ripois et la Némésis*.

What I gleaned from all these conversations and contacts, I carefully recorded in my thesis which consisted of three parts: a new biographical sketch of Louis Hémon in Paris and London (1880-1911), and a study of his early writings; a detailed account of his life in Canada (1911-13) and of all his writings about our country; and, finally, the extraordinary success story of *Maria Chapdelaine*, one of the best-sellers of the 20th century. On June 30, 1951, in a Sorbonne amphitheatre, I defended my work in a four-hour verbal joust with three professors, and was granted the degree of Docteur de l'Université de Paris.

Louis Hémon described Monsieur Ripois as having the 'ability to live by chapters.' In July 1951, I came to the end of the Parisian chapter of my life, and returned to my parents' home in Kingston after an absence of almost five years. The intensive work for my doctorate had exacted a heavy toll: I was physically exhausted, painfully thin, and suffering from severe eye strain. Both our family doctor and an eye specialist told me that I must rest for six months. I was allowed to use my eyes for close work only half an hour each day.

In November, I could stand the idleness no longer and came to Ottawa to look for work. Ottawa has been my home ever since. The eye specialist had advised me not to teach because of the long hours of preparation and correction, but to find employment in an office. I was offered three positions. How different from today when a graduate engineer living near us sent out five hundred résumés before finding work! After passing a written test, I was hired by the Bureau for Translations at an initial salary of $3,000, which was quite acceptable in those days. In order to be eligible, I had to demonstrate my ability to work in both directions, from English to French and from French to English. Because of my literary background, I was assigned to the External Affairs Division, where the material to be translated was less technical than elsewhere. I began work on December 3, 1951, and, in spite of several applications for posts in French Departments, the only university work I ever did was teaching an evening course at Carleton College in the summer of 1953. I remained a translator until April 18, 1961.

The thought of earning my living in this way had never crossed my mind, but there were compensations. In the first set of examinations after my arrival, I qualified as a Grade 4 translator, and my salary rose to about $4,200. When I resigned in 1961, it was almost $7,000 – an excellent income for a woman at that time. The External Affairs Division had a small staff: the chief, about six translators (French-Canadian and French), one stenographer and two typists. I was the only English-speaking person in the group. Not only did I sharpen my linguistic skills, both oral and written, but I thoroughly enjoyed the highly intellectual milieu and came to a better understanding of French-Canadian points of view. In the warm, family-like atmosphere, I made several close friends, some of whom I am still in touch with today.

The study of contemporary French literature had rekindled my interest in Christianity, and the 'Hound of Heaven' was still pursuing me. Francis Thompson's metaphor describes very aptly the inner compulsion I felt to identify myself formally with a church. But which church? I had drifted away from the United Church of Canada, in which I had been brought up, and had been strongly influenced by Roman Catholicism in France, at that time one of its most progressive branches. An Anglican friend had introduced me to the writings of C.S. Lewis. In Ottawa, I was finally attracted to Chalmers United Church by the preaching of the Rev Leonard Griffith. I explained my dilemma to him, and he responded: 'Try us for a while.' I took his advice, became a member of Chalmers Church in 1954, and am still there today. Basically, I remain the same, a strong believer in 'mere Christianity,' as C.S. Lewis expressed it, with little interest in denominations.

The decision was to have far-reaching consequences. Chalmers' dynamic deaconess, Miss Jessie MacLeod, invited me to participate in a panel presentation at the Young Adult Club, and I began to attend its activities. It was a kind of advanced Young People's Union for those in their twenties and thirties. The programme was a mixture of religious, social and recreational events. At the end of 1954, I was elected to the executive, served as worship convener for two years (1955-56), and then as president for two more (1957-58). These were my first ventures in Christian education, an area in which I still work today.

There are various pursuits: academic, professional, spiritual and ... matrimonial. As a witty friend observed, Audrey was looking for a free man! When I became president of the Young Adult Club, I said to myself: 'Well, if you ever expected to find a husband here, you may as well forget it. No man would ever marry Madam President.' I was mistaken. On the

Easter week-end of 1958, Gordon Campbell, one of the Club's programme conveners, offered me a drive to Kingston, where his sister and my parents lived. Outwardly, the trip was uneventful; inwardly, friendship exploded into love. Before a month had passed, we were discussing marriage, but we decided to wait for a year, just to be sure. Gordon gave me my engagement ring at Christmas 1958 and, on May 16, 1959, Madam President and the programme convener were married at Chalmers Church. It was the happiest day of my life. We are still happily married today.

Although Gordon was by profession a statistician, we have many common interests: theatre, music, ballet, cultural events in general, travelling. If I never became a feminist, it was probably because he was so supportive of all my undertakings. To help me meet my deadlines, he often does the household shopping and replaces me in the kitchen and the laundry-room. He has provided me with friendship as well as love, with complete financial and emotional security. How I wish that all women might be so fortunate!

Eight years had passed since 1951, when I had defended my thesis at the Sorbonne, and Louis Hémon had been pushed into the background. I had, however, used my first leave, in September 1952, to visit the Lake St John country. I had spent several days doing research in the archives at Chicoutimi, and had made my first pilgrimage to Péribonka and to the old Bédard farmhouse where Louis Hémon had gathered his material for *Maria Chapdelaine*. In 1960, I returned to the same area. Hémon's ghost continued to haunt me. Typed copies of my thesis had been given to the members of my jury and deposited in the Sorbonne library; several attempts to have it published had proved abortive. Shortly after my marriage, I was urged to revise it for publication, and was elated when the University of Toronto Press and the Presses Universitaires de France gave me a contract for a joint edition. In 1961, I resigned from my position as translator.

I now settled down in earnest to revise and update my thesis. I had a tiger by the tail. I had to take into account the books and articles that had appeared since 1951 on Louis Hémon. In addition, my style no longer satisfied me, and I found myself rewriting much of the text. My aim was to produce a book that would appeal to a wider public, less academic in character, as free as possible from footnotes. I was soon up to my ears in letters, index cards, interviews, articles, books and manuscript. I returned to France in 1964 and 1970, and each time saw Kitty Hémon again. In 1966, I had an enlightening interview with the widow of Clarence Gagnon, who illustrated the most famous edition of *Maria Chapdelaine*, published in 1933. The set of fifty-four original paintings had been bought by the late Col. R.S. (Sam) McLaughlin, Chairman of the Board of General Motors of Canada, in Oshawa, who showed them to Gordon and me when we visited him in 1966. They now form part of the McMichael Collection, at Kleinburg, near Toronto.

By this time, I had finished revising nine of the twelve chapters when a number of circumstances conspired to slow down, then to stop my work. In 1965 Gordon and I had become the parents of a little boy, Ian Bruce. My wedding day was the happiest day of my life; the second happiest was the day I became a mother. Ian was (and always has been) very active (my father nicknamed him Chain Lightning), and I felt as if I'd been put into orbit. I was not as successful as some other women at juggling child-rearing and writing. Things were further complicated by Gordon's poor health and by the new material on Louis Hémon that became available in the sixties.

The novelist's sister Marie, with whom I had lived in Paris, died in 1964 at the age of eighty-six, and, as often happens in such cases, the skeletons began to come out of the closet. In 1966, Kitty sold all the Hémon papers to the University of Montreal. Nicole Deschamps, who taught French there, published a letter from Louis Hémon to his father revealing what had been carefully concealed since 1913: Kitty's parents had not been married, and her mother, who had become mentally ill after Kitty's birth, had been confined to what was then called an asylum. Kitty had shown me this letter in 1964, shortly after discovering it, but, out of consideration for her feelings, I had not disclosed its contents.

In 1968, Nicole Deschamps also published *Louis Hémon: Lettres à sa famille*, an annotated edition of all the known letters sent by the writer to his family. The unpublished letters which I had appended to my thesis were no longer unpublished. Documents whose existence I hadn't even suspected had now to be taken into account. I was dismayed by the prospect of revising once again the chapters already completed. What a price I paid for having been unable to publish my thesis immediately after defending it! 'In disgrace with fortune and men's eyes,' as Shakespeare expressed it, I put the last chapter of my revised text in my desk drawer, where it still eyes me reproachfully.

After 1965, child-rearing occupied most of my time, and there was no doubt that Ian was now the centre of our household.

Gordon and I took him to the church school every Sunday morning, and, in 1969, I became a teacher. As I had only one child of my own, my church-school classes also represented for me a sort of enlarged family, and I still follow with interest their lives and careers. When other commitments made it necessary for me to resign in 1982 as superintendent of the Intermediate Department, I promoted into the communicants' class some students whom I had taught in the three-year-old nursery.

Chief among these other commitments was my work, from 1979 to 1986, as a United Church representative on the Inter-Church Committee on Christian Education. This Ottawa group, which seems to be unique in North America, is composed of representatives from nine denominations: the Anglican, Baptist, Lutheran, Mennonite, Presbyterian, Roman Catholic and United Churches, the Salvation Army and the Society of Friends. It organizes at least two events annually to provide training for church-school teachers and spiritual enrichment for parents and other concerned persons, and is an exciting example of the ecumenical coalitions among Christian denominations.

On this committee, I served as publicity convener from 1979 to 1982, as chairperson from 1982 to 1984, then as past chairperson. Being an ecumenical group, we were seconded to the first Canadian Christian Festival, held in Ottawa in May 1982, and helped to plan programs for about 13,000 children and youth over a four-day period. These were heavy responsibilities, but I grew intellectually and spiritually in that work more than in any other volunteer work that I have done. Finally, to help celebrate the fifteenth anniversary of the Committee's formation, I composed what became my swan song: a publicity brochure entitled 'The First Fifteen Years, 1971-1986.'

In 1980, the last revised chapter of my thesis on *Maria Chapdelaine* still lay undisturbed in my desk drawer, but Louis Hémon's ghost had not been laid. When I learned that the centenary of his birth was to be celebrated at Péribonka that August, in the presence of his daughter, I decided to go and write an article on the event for an Ontario newspaper. *The Globe and Mail* wasn't interested; nor were the two Ottawa English dailies. Not very hopefully, I phoned the Ottawa French-language paper, *Le Droit*, and was referred to the director of the literary page. Without promising to publish it, he offered to look at whatever I wrote. So, with this half-promise and armed, like Louis Hémon, with a notebook and a pencil, I set out for Péribonka.

It was a memorable event. The festivities lasted five days, from Wednesday, August 13, to Sunday, August 17.

On Saturday afternoon, to commemorate the crossing of Lake St John from Roberval to Péribonka by Louis Hémon in 1912, his daughter Lydia (Kitty to me) made the same trip on a tug of the Abitibi-Price Paper

Company. Later, the crowd moved on to 'les Aménagements Maria Chapdelaine,' which was merely a fancy name for the site of the old Bédard farm-house, a few miles to the east, for a 'souper populaire' featuring Lake St John dishes, followed by a programme starring local artists.

On Sunday morning, the Péribonka church was filled for the solemn mass celebrated and televised in memory of Louis Hémon. The walls of the apse bore quotations from *Maria Chapdelaine*, and the sermon was inspired by it. Louis Hémon would have been stupefied, for he was not a practising Roman Catholic, and went to mass only to appease his 'patronne,' Laura Bédard, and to take notes on the locals in a notebook, according to Laura, 'long comme le doigt.' No wonder the parish priest didn't like him! After mass, a local troupe re-enacted on the church steps the opening scene from the novel: news of the parish announced by the crier and the auctioning, not of a pig, as in the book, but of poultry, rabbits, blueberries and potatoes.

After our return to Ottawa, I prepared a long article on the centenary celebrations, 'Louis Hémon revit à Péribonka,' for the literary page of *Le Droit*. I had written hundreds of pages on Louis Hémon and *Maria Chapdelaine*; this was the first to appear in print.

Since the centenary, there has been a veritable explosion of events related to Louis Hémon and his Canadian novel, and I have been invited to attend, or to participate in, almost all of them. On October 12, 1981, Alain Stanké's Montreal publishing house launched a sumptuous album, *Jean Paul Lemieux retrouve Maria Chapdelaine*. I also went to a symposium on the novelist held in May 1982 at Alma, near Lake St John, and at Péribonka. The following year, *Maria Chapdelaine* really made the headlines when Gilles Carle, a well-known French Canadian producer, brought out a greatly overrated film version of the novel. It was produced both in French and in English, and there was also a TV mini-series, in both languages. In this same period, I continued to visit with Kitty at Quimper, in Brittany, and she, in Ottawa, with us. I also had interviews with three illustrators of *Maria Chapdelaine*: Thoreau MacDonald and Jean Paul Lemieux, in Canada; Sylvain Hairy, in France. Another interview was with Lewis Pagé, a talented sculptor from Quebec City, who had created for the centenary a striking bronze bust of Louis Hémon.

When, in 1985, the city of Quimper, the Department of Finistère and the Province of Quebec sponsored in Brittany an 'Hommage à Louis Hémon,' I was invited to give a paper at the symposium which was one of the highlights of a varied cultural programme. Twelve French and Canadian participants spoke on a variety of subjects: *Maria Chapdelaine*;

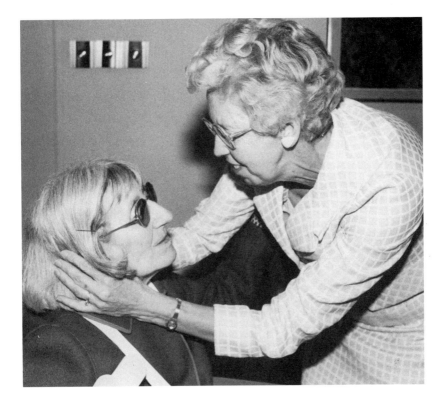

Lydia ("Kitty") Hémon, welcomed by Audrey Campbell at Mirabel on June 1, 1986, en route to Péribonka for the opening of the new Musée Louis-Hémon. CREDIT: Bernard Brault, La Presse.

the sports articles and stories by Louis Hémon; the film based on the London novel, *Monsieur Ripois et la Némésis*; Hémon's paternal ancestry; the Louis Hémon Museum. I was the only woman to give a paper, and the only participant whose mother tongue was English. Under the title, 'Louis Hémon vu par Jacques de Marsillac,' I drew a portrait of the writer based on the reminiscences of his most intimate friend in London, who later became the editor of *Le Journal*, a large Paris daily.

The 'Hommage à Louis Hémon' was a worthy prelude to an extremely important event: the official opening of the Musée Louis-Hémon at Péribonka on June 5, 1986. This crowned six years of unswerving tenacity on the part of the curator, Gilbert Lévesque. The museum is a handsome building of modern design, white to symbolize the snow, with large windows on its curving façade which, like *Maria Chapdelaine*, reflect the changing seasons. After passing through the outer entrance, visitors walk through the wooden doors of the old Péribonka church which Louis Hémon knew.

The next day, in the presence of Kitty Hémon, the name 'Mont Louis-Hémon' was officially conferred on a mountain situated on the north-east shore of Lake Jacques Cartier in the Parc des Laurentides, between Lake St John and Quebec City. In the evening, I repeated the lecture that I had given the previous October in Brittany.

Almost forty years have passed since I was awarded the Marty and, looking back, I feel that life has been very good to me. I'm deeply grateful for the scholarships that made it possible for me to spend close to five years in France, five years of 'French immersion.' Knowing two languages is like leading two lives; a second language opens the door to another mode of life and thought. I treasure my friendships in France and French Canada. Did I choose my thesis subject, or did it choose me? There was something almost inevitable about it. Once chosen, it took control of my life; I have still not escaped from it.

Like many university graduates today, I never found the work for which I had prepared myself and, as a translator, I used only part of my training. My volunteer work in Christian education, however, has always been very satisfying. Through it, I met my husband and became a 'compleat' woman: a wife and a mother. I have never lost interest in Louis Hémon and *Maria Chapdelaine*. Since the centenary in 1980 of the novelist's birth, there has been a tremendous resurgence of interest in him, and once again the 'divinity that shapes our ends' is drawing me back into the circle of Louis Hémon specialists. In 1948, the Marty found me just beginning my research on *Maria Chapdelaine*. The 50th anniversary of the scholarship, in 1987, sees me still following the same star, which has indeed guided me 'from Paris to Péribonka.'

In retrospect

Doreen Maxwell Hotchkiss

Am I a scholar? Just to be certain of the definition, I reached for the Oxford Dictionary ... not an easy thing to reach for in the average household south of the Forty-Ninth Parallel. In our house it has long been viewed with suspicion. That book? That's the one Mum uses to 'prove she's right.' I found to my surprise that, au contraire, I fit in my own mind the definitions given for scholar seventy-five per cent of the time! Viz ... a pupil, one who is taught in school; one who studies in the schools of a university; a student who receives emoluments during a fixed period from the funds of a school, college or university; a learned or erudite person. The last one was the rub and the one I protested. I am by no means a learned person. Well educated? Reasonably intelligent? Yes. Erudite? No. Have I made a medical breakthrough, devised a new mathematical formula, found what is on beyond the prior or provided proof of a fifth dimension? None of these. I am a person who is wandering into her sixtieth year looking back over her shoulder to what? No rockets or flares, no Nobel prizes ... but there are four marvellous young people in their twenties spinning off into their own futures, a wonderful classically absent-minded professor husband, a mass of research data waiting to be drawn to its logical conclusion and published. There is also a pile of mugs and humorously assorted plaques ... 'for stimulating the minds of young boys,' 'for exemplary service and personal sacrifice on behalf of her colleagues and students,' 'Teacher of the Year for Kentucky' ... actually one-sixth of teacher of the year since the University of Kentucky chooses six from the University and its Community Colleges ... 'Teacher of the Year for a Community College.' Not exactly top-level stuff.

I actually feel ridiculously proud and busy and happy and unapologetic. Perhaps, after all, there is a place for the 'unsung' scholar in its widest sense, for the wife of twenty-nine years, the mother, the researcher and the teacher.

Doreen Maxwell Hotchkiss

Roots? Heavily Canadian. My mother's people came from England, Ireland and Scotland to Ontario to the Ottawa Valley region. My father's came from Scotland, to the Maritimes directly or indirectly as United Empire Loyalists from the future States. Secondarily many moved up to the Ottawa Valley. My maternal grandfather was the restless one in his family who left the farm, taught himself telegraphy, ran the wireless office, clerked in a store, bought it, became enamoured of the future of the automobile, had two of the first garages and dealerships in his area and was mayor of his town half his life. My maternal grandmother attended Ottawa Normal and taught in the same small town, riding her bicycle in long skirts, defying gravity to the entrancement of her future husband. My paternal grandfather was a teacher and principal of a high school academy who decided to 'take law' at McGill when his children were half-grown. He became a legend in small towns along the Ottawa and a powerful prosecutor. His wife had been brought up 'delicately' in a town family.

It was as inevitable as death and taxes that I go to Queen's. My parents were Queen's graduates; my father's oldest sister, much later her two daughters and a son of one of the daughters were Queen's graduates; my mother's younger brother and later his son were Queen's graduates. We've lost count of those less closely related. My parents, although both were living in the same small town of Vankleek Hill, met at Queen's when my father returned from four years in World War I. Taught by his father, he had finished high school and gone overseas at the age of sixteen with his father's unwilling permission. He was allowed to drive trains up to No-Man's-Land to carry back the wounded until he was considered old enough to fight. His family's finances had taken a setback and on his return, instead of pursuing the law degree he had his heart set on, he went into Civil Engineering. He arranged with Dean Ellis to work on highways until winter set in and then each year to join the courses that were by then underway, for as long as his grades kept up. His grades kept up and so did his social life. Law may have been his dream but engineering was an excellent substitute. He was a trouble shooter who recognized a problem, designed a solution for roads or dams or paper mills and, once a problem was solved, was off to new horizons. My mother completed her BA Honours in three years and chose marriage over a Master's degree. They moved swiftly and frequently, from Temiskaming to Edmunston to Olean, NY, to Puerto Rico to Pongo, Bolivia, within the next five years and continued moving for the next thirty years. An hilariously stimulating couple, they were socially exceedingly active as well, much more so than their only child. I often felt, breathlessly, that I was being pulled along after them in the mode of Alice in Wonderland, feet rarely touching the ground. I seldom spent more than one year at a time in a school until I was stashed away with my grandmother while my father went overseas for the second time. Actually my early schooling was a challenge in itself with exposure to different teachers, different teaching methods and different school mates. I never did learn the counties of Ontario but I read John Buchan's *Thirty-Nine Steps* three times in different classes and *Midsummer Night's Dream* five times. I missed early geometry, yet was catapulted into Newfoundland schools where they had already had algebra for two years.

Most of my high school years were at Vankleek Hill Collegiate Institute, small, comfortable and excellent. There I took all the Grade Thirteen subjects. I did not want to go to Queen's because I felt that I could never live up to the academic and social reputations engendered there by my parents. Trying to flunk out of high school, however, seemed a bit too radical a step.

A loving principal had me groomed to apply for scholarships. I won one in biology. Although I had planned on a classical English-History future, who was I to quibble with fate? What was meant to be, would be. I would be a scientist! Ha! 'There were manys the slip' in this decision. My background was weak in mathematics and physics and chemistry. In my pursuit of science I eventually attacked and swallowed biology but encompassed only as much of the others as the course requirements demanded. This has been a lifetime hindrance. Gradually, I have compensated enough to do my own research and understand that of others, although my comprehension in math and physics has remained elementary.

The first year at Queen's I began to think might be my last. Dr John Stanley, back from the War, was an excellent Invertebrate Zoologist and a perfectionist. He did not take kindly to the treatment his equipment had been given in his absence and felt the calibre of students had taken a plunge as well. He was sure of it when I showed up in class, a country mouse who did not know one end of a microscope from the other. I spent many sessions with Jean Royce trying to squirm out of his class but she finally incited some spunk in me. My triumph came when he gave a second set of exams because I had aced the first set and he was sure something was wrong with the test itself. This minor victory seemed to mark a turning point. The Lord helps those who help themselves and even if I had not actually been ear-marked by fate for biology, I might as well accept it as a challenge and lick it.

There were one or two brief flurries towards veterinary medicine or medicine itself. Unfortunately I discovered that I lost not only my equilibrium but several meals every time I bent over a living anesthetized dog. This might have passed, but I doubt it. I detest heights and have clambered innumerable ladders and peered over countless cliffs and have become neither cured nor efficient. Discretion therefore seemed the better part of valour and I looked for the parts of the living world where I could work with enthusiasm and excitement.

Another discovery was that I preferred instant gratification. I favoured morphological and anatomical studies, detailed work I could control with my hands and see with my eyes (even if aided by microscopes), over mysteries of long-term culture rearings. I found too that I could become lyrically drunk with theorizing and hypothesizing and that it was all too easy to develop a passion for the unknowns of embryological development, for the mysteries of metamorphosis and the black holes of knowledge of cell structure and function.

My first summer, I began working at the Experimental Farm in Ottawa in Entomology. Working at the Insectory feeding thousands of tiny larvae which were funneled in from rangers all over the country may not seem the cream of the employment world, but it was fun. I learned a lot and research projects galore presented themselves free for the picking. We developed our preferences. Mine was a group of primitive Hymenopteran sawflies that presented some fascinating morphological and systematic puzzles. After completing ministudies on some representative species, I strong-armed Dr Allen West into allowing me to use the material for a Master's research project, funded by a Queen's Reuben Wells Leonard Resident Fellowship.

The Master's program was exciting and fun and culminated in my one and only (so far) 'book.' This was an entire issue of the *Canadian Entomologist* and was devoted to the comparative internal anatomy of the larvae of as many families and genera and species of sawflies as I had then obtained. Definitely not a book of the month choice, never on the best-seller lists, it has, however, kept turning over and there continues to be a slow trickle of requests from China, Japan, and Russia, of all places.

Another turning point seemed to be in the offing. The entire scientific method was becoming addictive. There is something dangerously heady in discovering something that no one else has known. I was feeling the urge to extend horizons to include other organisms besides the insects.

By this time, in my off-school time, I had been transferred to Sault Ste. Marie as an assistant to an English insect cytogeneticist who could get chromosomes out of a stone. The lab was a Forest Entomology headquarters and the incoming insect material was endless.

I was receiving some invaluable field training in genetics and cytogenetics and wanted more. With the help of an Ontario Research Fellowship to the Department of Genetics, I went on to McGill and, in some ways, started over. Taking every undergrad and graduate course in the department and in some neighbouring departments, was stimulating but not easy. I did not shine as a newly hatched star on their horizon but I did emerge with a remarkably able background in cytology and in all aspects of genetics, including human genetics. As my doctoral research was cytogenetic studies of my sawflies, I needed to work with a woman cytogeneticist who had turned out the early and only work of sawfly chromosomes.

Dr Ann Sanderson was at University College, Dundee, a branch of St Andrews. I applied for help and received the honour of Queen's Marty Memorial Scholarship and a Canadian Federation of University Women's Travelling Scholarship. Packing up a suitcase of sawfly cocoons of various species that were supposed to mature slowly and be available for cytological preparations during the winter, and accompanied by a permit from the Department of Agriculture, I sailed for unsuspecting Scotland. The cocoons started to hatch in Montreal with the buzzing accompaniment of the females' ovipositors which gave them their name. They continued to hatch with an increasing frenzy. I created a colonial sensation on a train from Glasgow to Dundee. I had an overnight bag with a ticking alarm clock and the suitcase of insects liberally plastered with 'BEWARE, LIVE MATERIAL' signs. The clock ticked, the bag buzzed. Fellow passengers in my compartment began to move away and I was politely removed from the train to provide lengthy explanations.

The year in Scotland was a revelation. It was a complete exposure to a different academic atmosphere, a different pace, and to people whose research approach reflected entirely different educational backgrounds. It was a wonderful year. Besides working with an extraordinarily fine group of people at Dundee, I spent time in Biology and Genetics Departments at Edinburgh, Glasgow and Aberdeen. The British Museum's sawfly authority, a delightful Dr Benson, visited Dundee and I trotted all over after him on field trips. In the Spring I spent a few weeks working with him at the British Museum. I was given access to a mass of unworked collections of Australian sawflies that made me 'drool.' It was the Spring of the Coronation and London was *the* place in the world to be.

Whenever I began to feel that it was not merely supreme good fortune that brought this all on, but that possibly I was a genius ... something, fortunately, would happen to restore my commonsense and bring me down to earth with a bang. For instance, while I was nervously addressing a prestigious group of Scottish Lions Club representatives on the Canadian Forestry Division and its problems, for support I kept my eye on an elderly gentleman in the front row. He beamed at me, nodded his head sagely at every point I made and restored my confidence no end. I felt I must be God's gift to ambassadorship. When I finished, he rushed up, pumped my hand and said, 'Dearrie ... I dinna kent a worrd ye said. I'm deaf as a post, but ye've a bonnie face tha' reminds me o' my own bairn.'

Back in Montreal it was time to wrap up 'prelims' and begin the thesis round-up. I joined a number of PhDs in Genetics and Cytology who received their degrees on the eve of the breakthrough of DNA. It meant that everything we had done and studied had to be re-evaluated. What we could see in our cytological preparations were like dark ages sightings compared to what the electron microscope could show. It was time to start all over again. While I was polishing my thesis, Dr West left on sabbatical and I took over his classes. A fascinating experience it was to be back teaching in my alma mater with the friendly support of those who had been my mentors.

The next year I went off to Australia as a National Research Council Postdoctoral Fellow. If any biologist is to be given a taste of heaven on earth, send her or him to Australia. Explosions of long-isolated flora and fauna produce such a wealth of material, such bizarre forms, such ranges of variability, that I felt that I should begin all over again in interpreting my pet group. I loved every minute of my year there and, apart from my work, I was exceedingly interested in educational backgrounds and teaching techniques and comparisons with Scotland and home. I acquired magnificent material in the field, untold quantities for future work.

The prize collection, however, turned out to be an American Botany Professor who had been teaching at the University of Sydney and doing research for five years. He was about to return to the University of Louisville in the United States. He must have been ready to settle down because he had withstood approaches by an enormous female contingent at the University of Sydney. I had two advantages. I knew all the American songs when we were off on field trips, perhaps a nostalgic advantage over *Waltzing Matilda*, and I slowly and insidiously started helping him with his cytological preparations. This could possibly have been *his* Tom Sawyer fence white-washing technique, of course. I impressed him also by insisting upon carrying my own collecting equipment. Slender strands to bind a couple together! A long-term love-affair with Australia is something we have always shared. 'Hotch' returned to a spring semester at Louisville, dithered and finally left a letter for the departmental secretary to mail. The letter was a proposal which was supposed to reach me in Sydney but finally caught up at the port of Bombay. Meanwhile I had cabled acceptance from Ceylon to the University of New Brunswick to teach in the Biology Department there. The year in New Brunswick was stimulating and practical. Time to pull together postdoctoral research, time to organize my own teaching techniques, time to get ready for whatever the future had in store.

We were married the following spring and spent the first few years' vacation times collecting Charophytes (one of my husband's special interests, a group of green algae) around the countryside. We were collaborating with a foremost charologist, Wood, at the University of Rhode Island, doing his chromosome work, and wandering up and down the Ottawa and St Lawrence Rivers and the Niagara Peninsula following old collecting reports from the last century, searching out the old species for re-examination and cytological work. Visits to our respective families in Canada and New York State were punctuated by making cytological preparations in their bathrooms and kitchens. Very shortly, since we produced four young in five years, we filled their homes with disposable diapers as well.

The number four astonished and perturbed some members of my husband's department. We were at the height of 'population crisis awareness' and should only have produced 1.5 offspring! The same five years were illuminating if somewhat vague. Academically I kept abreast of current literature and continued to do my husband's chromosome preps in the kitchen. We were collaborating with several groups who forwarded material to us for cytological examination, and he and his graduate students made constant field trips in and out of state, increasing the work to be done. Mostly, however, I ran a home nursery, or so it seemed with our eventual four. I loved every minute of it but I was never entirely awake. We talked, we read, we hiked, we painted, we had tea parties, we were creative, we were destructive ... all of it.

The next five years were somewhat similar, but expanded somewhat academically. Despite being very conscious of the dangers of nepotism, the University of Louisville let me teach a course in Genetics and one in

Entomology, when they were suddenly in need. Once the kindergarten-first-grade-second-grade programs began, life expanded into a carpooling morass and the duties, voluntary, of being a cloakroom aide (that is, carrying everything from crystal gardens to dead cats to schools to supplement programs). Kentucky public schools were forty-eighth or forty-ninth in degree of academic excellence and in the throes of horribly administered innovative attempts to improve. We implemented, supplemented and fought schemes, working quietly on the sidelines, to keep our four and their classmates on an even educational keel. Two summers were spent at the University of Oklahoma's Biology Station on Lake Texoma. My husband taught Botany and the five of us scoured the country for fossils, retraced old pony express routes, and cavorted with armadillos. We all got together 'after hours' and on weekends for swimming, trips down into Texas and more researching.

When our youngest was going-on five and our oldest was going-on ten, we drove to California in January, left our car with friends and took a liner for Australia for a sabbatical leave of my husband's. The University of Sydney provided temporary university housing until we found a tiny old world house in a suburb of Lane Cove a few hundred yards from hiking trails along the shores of Sydney Harbour. The four were inserted into an excellent public school where they had the best teaching they had ever had or were ever to have. We bought a car for the year and travelled widely, renewing old habitats and old friendships and exposing the children to the wonders of the Australian wilderness. We collected, we cytologized and my husband lectured some in his old Department. Before leaving, we took a train far up the coast to spend a week on Heron Island on the Great Barrier Reef at a Biology Station. When you have assisted a giant sea turtle in laying her eggs, have been nipped by a mutton bird, hissed over by an emu and kicked gently by a wallaby, Australia tends to assume the characteristics of one gloriously large zoo. It was most reluctantly that our four allowed themselves to be transported away from that great southern continent.

Back in the US, home continued to be a site for subsidizing the local school system. The children throve and were in advanced programs but the 'advanced' worried us because, with the rare exceptional class, they were getting very little. We continued volunteering madly and interfering constantly to see that no stone was left unturned in the work they did to get the most out of what was there. Their father included them in field trips. We backed the Cub Scouts and the Boy Scouts and should have given equal time to the two girls. We tried.

During the last fifteen years, while their schooling was progressing, I began part-time teaching at Indiana University Southeast, just across the Ohio River from us, in entomology, invertebrate zoology and introductory biology or ecology. Very little time was involved and the home fires kept burning. I found myself shockingly successful. I could handle a class of up to eighty non-science majors; I could get even the most reluctant excited enough to want more; and I could teach to almost complete comprehension. A combination of scandalous data, humorous facts and an old-fashioned teaching technique, returning to a stage where there was no information on a topic and bringing them up to the current status as if they were part of it, worked. I had them coming back for more and I enjoyed it thoroughly.

Ten years ago, with the oldest in university and the other three in high school, I took on the first 'full-time' job of my married life as the biology teacher for a newly established private high school. What I had not already learned about young people, I was to find out. The 'children' were sophisticated young with highly active social lives who cared not a whit for academia. Their parents expected four years would see their little angels accepted at Harvard and Yale. I swore, at first, that Godiva riding into class on her white horse could not have made a dint on my blasé students. Gradually, with a combination of mothering and yelling, they let me teach, and, eventually, most responded by being able to test out of their chosen universities in freshman biology courses.

After four years, I joined a community college with a new campus in a self-described 'blue-collar' area. Here, for entirely different reasons, the students were a real challenge. Many were much older, mothers with young children desperate to get work and needing a career; men out of work, needing some kind of academic advancement to get back into a work force; people with backgrounds needing an incredible amount of remedial work. These were men and women with families grown wanting to take a step they were not able to take years before.

In an attempt to bridge the gap between high school and college, I set up free Human Ecology courses on Saturday mornings for high school sophomores, juniors and seniors. My aim was that they be exposed to college and develop environmental awareness. Since I did not want tuition to be a discriminating factor, funding has been one of my major concerns. I have been funded by a foundation once and an ecologically minded couple twice but the other times I have funded myself. As one reporter put it 'Teacher pays students to take her class!' It's a program I am vitally interested in. I have seen it turn perfectly unaware, ecologically blind high schoolers into concerned, aware, ecologically minded citizens. I am currently trying to persuade University of Louisville ecologists to take over the program because the University could afford to waive the students' tuition.

Every student has been a friend and a personal problem. Sometimes, I have been able to help; sometimes I have just been able to listen. Always I have given them course contents they could handle and use. This has been a very down-to-earth activity, no different from what every teacher does and has done from the beginning of time. Every student and his or her future has been a challenge. It is like having an ever-expanding family.

I have always been much more interested in teaching Biology and Human Genetics than in fighting for Women's Rights for two reasons. I insist that a 'shoemaker should stick to his last.' I am much better equipped to fight for ecological and genetic awareness than to protest the hiring and firing of women, salary ranges, or academic credibility. I was well aware that I could teach part-time forever at Indiana University but that in a male-dominated science department I would never be accepted full-time regardless of my academic qualifications. I was well aware that students tended to accept the sciences from a male instructor more open-mindedly than from a female instructor. I have even traitorously recommended the hiring of a male physics teacher over a female at my hard-core community college for the sake of student acceptance. As a visiting or resident alien, my second reason for acting passively is that I have felt it *not my* inalienable right to tackle these issues in the United States.

Being a Canadian living in the United States has rarely proved difficult. I have tended to be on my best behaviour and my 'fellow Americans' have as well. One pseudo-serious confrontation arose when, having been a Den Mother for four years, I was 'exposed' by one of the Boy Scout Council administrators as being an alien. I was called in for an interview and told that I was unsuitable as a Den Mother because I was not an American citizen. I protested and he said 'My dear lady (lower case), what, for example, do you do with your hands when they play *The Star-Spangled Banner?*' I thought at first it was some sort of trick question but finally admitted that indeed, I did not hold my hand over my heart. I insisted that I *did* stand at attention out of respect and taught my cubs what to do with *their* hands. The whole case went as far as Washington and blew over when a letter back suggested that if they had any female 'damn fool enough to want to continue to be a Den Mother,' they should hold on to her even if she were from outer space.

Our four offspring have been our unfinished but oh-so-promising theses. We consider them to be our best claims to fame and our holds on the future. They grew up in the Sixties and Seventies and emerged happy, balanced, ambitious, humorous individuals who can view drugs and alcohol dispassionately and look at sex responsibly. What more can we ask? They view us with loving, amused tolerance as living anachronisms and they do not take themselves too seriously.

A year ago Christmas, my husband's retirement was precipitated by the onset of Parkinsonism and a mild stroke. Our priorities shifted considerably. By summer his health became generally regulated. His freedom, though, has been severely cut and his health needs to be carefully supervised. He decided to give up driving and expose himself to my tender mercies as his chauffeuse. His fine manipulatory movements of writing and typing are slowed and we make more progress if we work together. I am determined to maintain a regimen that keeps his sense of humour functioning, that makes him feel needed and important. So far three papers are off 'in press' and two more are coming out of the wings. When we finish writing up all the unfinished papers, we are going to continue one or two pet projects where his research is teetering on the brink of some fascinating breakthroughs. We also want to start pulling masses of his notes together into a long, only half-seriously proposed book on plant geography. Meanwhile, I am teaching this final year to get some programs well established and I will retire next spring. On the side, I hope to pull together all my own sidetracked insect research and start organizing notes for my own dream book on human genetics. One of the first topics for it we are already researching – Parkinson's Disease.

The song writer Stevie Wonder when asked, 'What is your favourite song?,' answered 'I haven't written it yet.' Ask me what I consider my major accomplishment as a Queen's graduate and a Marty Scholar, and perhaps I'll say that with the exception of finding one wonderful husband and producing four wonderful children, I haven't done it yet.

Go East young woman

BARBARA EXCELL HAWGOOD

I belong to the first generation of New Zealand women who could travel relatively cheaply and easily across the world. It is the story of my travels and of the universities in which I have studied that I wish to tell.

I entered Canterbury College of the University of New Zealand in 1947 to study science. My interest soon focussed on the life sciences, particularly mammalian physiology and biochemistry and I later transferred to Otago University (University of New Zealand) where these science subjects were taught in association with the Medical School. Otago University has many similarities with Queen's University. The province of Otago in the southern region of the South Island (furthest from the equator) was chosen in 1844 for a Scottish settlement. As in Canada, the settlers brought their distinctive Scots tradition of education and were proud that their ancient universities were attended by a higher proportion of the population than in any other European country at this time.

When I entered Otago University in 1949, the Head of the Physiology Department was Professor J.C. Eccles, FRS (later Sir John), one of the most productive and prolific contributors to neuroscience in this century. Professor Eccles had the intense intellectual drive, physical stamina and enthusiasm possessed by great scientists. Unbeknown to me, he was also poised for a major scientific breakthrough. His great interest was in the mechanisms of excitation and inhibition in the central nervous system. It was well established that, in the peripheral nervous system, excitatory transmission from nerve to muscle cell or from nerve to nerve cell was by chemical means. However, there was no convincing evidence that this was so in the central nervous system and Professor Eccles had published an ingenious model in which electrical events were the basis of both excitatory and inhibitory transmission. He expounded his model with great clarity and enthusiasm but rigorous testing depended upon the successful insertion of a microelectrode into the interior of a spinal motoneurone, a technique then in its infancy. The decisive test to show unequivocally that inhibitory transmission was not electrical came in August 1951 after I had left Otago University. Professor Eccles continued his work at the Australian National University, Canberra, and in 1963 he received the Nobel Prize for Physiology and Medicine jointly with A.F. Huxley and A.L. Hodgkin of Cambridge University, England.

On Professor Eccles' recommendation, I applied for the post of Demonstrator in Physiology in the University of Queensland, Australia and, after graduating, travelled to Brisbane in January 1951. In comparison with the small islands of New Zealand with their vertical contours and still active volcanic region, Australia is an ancient land of horizontal perspective. In Queensland, volcanic cores rise abruptly and weirdly from an eroded landscape. A reminder of the geological past was the strange grove within a rain forest isolated on a plateau south of Brisbane. I vividly remember the huge Antarctic beech, their branches festooned with lichen, appearing like botanical versions of the ancient mariner forever telling their tale. Queensland is a vast state and, as in the nineteenth century it was still a rural frontier, its university was not founded until 1909, the 50th anniversary of the state's independence. Completion of a fine university campus was slow and, during my stay, the life sciences remained scattered and relatively isolated although the Physiology building itself was centrally situated and close to the Botanical Gardens and the river. Departmental research included physiological studies on imported Zebu cattle to help assess their suitability for introduction into the hot Queensland outback; the tropic of Capricorn is just 350 miles north of Brisbane. From 1951 to 1953, I undertook teaching duties and research for an MSc degree on the subject of the influence of hormonal deficiencies on iron absorption from the small intestine.

As the work approached completion, it was natural that I should wish to travel further afield. I was a third generation Australasian and the physical isolation of the two countries made us very aware of and interested in the outside world. I decided to go eastward to Canada and wrote letters of enquiry to the University of British Columbia and Queen's University. In the event, I accepted the post of Research Assistant to Dr R.E. Semple at Queen's and, in the early summer of 1954, I sailed to Vancouver as an immigrant.

For two months I worked in the Rockies at Jasper and Lake Louise, and from this stay I have retained a love of great, bow-shaped glacial valleys and aquamarine-tinted moraine lakes and a mild abhorrence of coffee urns. My eastward journey by Canadian Pacific Railway from Banff

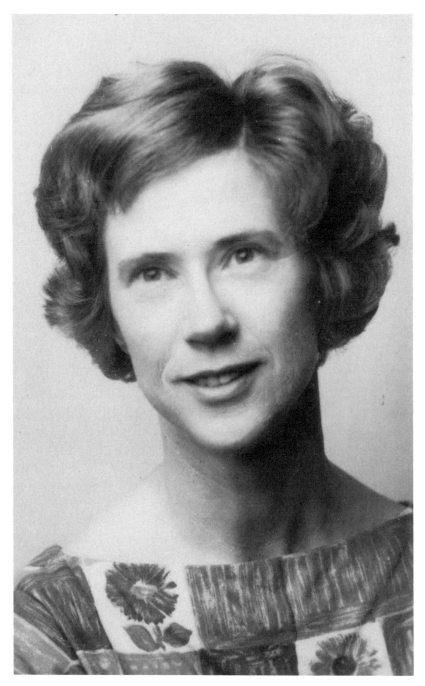

Barbara Excell Hawgood, London, 1962

to Toronto showed me the beauties of the Canadian Shield country for the first time, although delight at the unbelievably brilliant colours of autumn was yet to come. In Kingston I was given a warm welcome by Bob Semple and, under his guidance, commenced a study of the metabolic breakdown of dextran, the new plasma expander which had been extensively used in the treatment of shock in the recent Korean war. Two years later, I commenced work for my PhD on the bleeding disorder induced by dextran. The mid-fifties was a time of expansion of the Department and I duly moved to the well-equipped laboratories of the new Physiology building. The post-graduate school at Queen's was remarkably international at this time and included a considerable number of British graduates, many of whom came to work with Professor J.K.N. Jones, a British carbohydrate chemist who held the Chown Research Chair. Many of us were subjects in a research project on the relationship of diet to blood fat levels. I dutifully consumed a liquid diet (chocolate or strawberry flavoured) and at regular intervals presented myself for blood sampling, quite oblivious, in this double blind trial, as to whether I was in the corn oil group in which blood cholesterol was found to be quickly lowered or in the butter fat group in which blood cholesterol was observed to rise sharply.

My introduction to Canadian football was in the heady days when the Golden Gaels were intercollegiate champions and I joined in the chants with great enthusiasm. For the latter part of my PhD, I resided in Ban Righ. Here I came to know Dr Alice Vibert Douglas, Dean of Women, and formed a friendship which has provided me with continual encouragement and widening interests over thirty years. Three images particularly remind me of this period: talking with the Douglas family on the verandah of their cottage in the Thousand Islands, drinking Earl Grey tea with Dr Douglas in her room in Ban Righ and glimpsing the beauty of the stained glass windows of Chartres Cathedral from a transparent card affixed to one of her window panes.

As I was nearing completion of the work for my thesis, my interest in blood coagulation prompted me to write to Dr R.G. Macfarlane, FRS, of the Department of Haematology, Radcliffe Infirmary, Oxford. I was accepted for post-doctoral study if I could support myself. At the end of 1958, I applied for the Marty Travelling Scholarship, completed my PhD and sailed from San Francisco to New Zealand to see my parents. In Christchurch I received word that I had been awarded the Scholarship and, with heartfelt thanks to Queen's women, I sailed eastwards once more, but this time to England.

With some trepidation I started my journey from Southampton to Oxford. I had received no word from Oxford since my initial correspondence over a year previous, but I thrilled to the taxi ride in London over Westminster Bridge, past the Houses of Parliament, the Royal Parks, Buckingham Palace and Marble Arch to Paddington station, and next day found that I was quite expected in the Oxford laboratory! I found central lodgings in Springfield St Mary, a Victorian hostel run by a working order of Anglican nuns as part of St Anne's College.

Oxford gave me my first real sense of history. One day I idly noted that North Parade was further south than South Parade, a few blocks away. On being told that at one stage of the Civil War, North Parade was the northern limit of King Charles' men whereas South Parade marked the southern limit of Cromwell's army, a whole era of history became alive.

In my work, I was particularly interested to determine how the structure of the formed blood clot as shown by its tensile strength was affected in the various bleeding disorders, an aspect that I had studied for the dextran-induced condition. These changes turned out to be relatively minor, confirming that the fault lay in the slowed rate of formation of the fibrin strands. At the end of my year at Oxford I returned to the mainstream of cardiovascular physiology, accepting a post in the Department of Neuropathology, Institute of Psychiatry, University of London. The project concerned the identification of the areas of the brain that were vulnerable to damage as the result of a profound fall in blood pressure as may occur during certain operations.

Living in a high density area in south-east London was a new experience and one day I confessed to Dr Douglas, who was on one of her many visits, that I was not sure if I enjoyed London. She replied, 'It's impossible not to enjoy London,' and listed the riches to be had within a thirty-minute bus ride. I really agreed and after 26 years of living in London still do so; nevertheless I was grateful for this timely encouragement. After my research grant terminated in 1962 I joined the academic staff of Queen Elizabeth College, University of London.

Queen Elizabeth College was formerly King's College of Household and Social Science for Women which, in turn, had evolved from King's College for Women. In the late nineteenth century King's College (London) had favoured separate education for men and women and the women's college taught a wide range of arts and science subjects in Kensington. As with most institutions, however, King's evolved with the needs of society. In 1908 a Department of Household Science was inaugurated to give systematic instruction in home science, including the application of chemistry to food and of biology, physiology and bacteriology to sanitation and hygiene.

At the turn of the century, infant mortality was high in London and John Atkins, a house physician at Guy's Hospital just south of the City of London, was dismayed by the poor ill-nourished children entering the hospital and the general ignorance of the mothers as to the care of their children. He was immensely interested that home science subjects be taught to all young girls and became a staunch advocate of the Home Science Department of King's College for Women. From these early initiatives, Queen Elizabeth College developed into a small coherent community within the University of London, specializing in the Life Sciences. The first Department of Nutrition in Britain was established there in 1954 and, soon after, separate departments of biochemistry and microbiology were formed. The College continued to expand its flourishing research school, latterly encompassing biotechnology.

In the Physiology Department of Queen Elizabeth College, I once more commenced teaching and my research interests took yet another turn. This period marked the start of a technological explosion and expansion of medical research so that specialized equipment for electrophysical recording was now commercially available. I took up the challenge and commenced intracellular micro-electrode recording from the neuromuscular junction of single muscle fibres using the powerful technique pioneered by Professor Eccles. My aim was the study of certain neurotoxic snake venoms. The use of pharmacological substances to interfere with and reveal physiological processes had been known for a long time. Drugs extracted from plants had been crucial to the demonstration that neuromuscular transmission was chemical in nature. However, the use of neurotoxins of animal origin was just beginning. Professor C.Y. Lee of the National University of Taiwan had recently shown that a protein isolated from the venom of the Formosan krait irreversibly blocked acetylcholine receptors at the neuromuscular junction (thus leading to the death of the victim). Later this neurotoxin was successfully exploited to give new information about these receptors.

Initially my post-graduate students and I examined some of the components of the Cape cobra and Jameson's mamba venoms. Later I started work in collaboration with Professor Oswaldo Vital Brazil of the State University of Campinas, Sao Paulo, Brazil, on the mode of action of crotoxin, a neurotoxin that he had isolated from the venom of the deadly South American rattlesnake. This we showed to interfere with the release of neurotransmitter from motor nerve terminals. Shortly afterwards

I was invited to work for several months in Campinas and travelled briefly in Brazil, Peru and Venezuela; it was a fascinating experience. Although my current research has changed from time to time with the study of different neurotoxins on different types of excitable membrane, I periodically return to the study of transmitter release which still holds so many of its secrets.

Nineteen seventy-four saw my marriage to David and an even greater enjoyment of life. In August 1985, as part of the current reorganization of the University of London, Queen Elizabeth College was reunited with King's College. A new era has begun.

Part Two

1959–1987

A slow awakening

Elspeth Wallace Baugh

The request to reminisce about my life has forced me to reflect upon my own progression from an unaware, satisfied and privileged young woman to a more aware, unapologetic feminist who is still satisfied with her own life, but not with the lives of many women I know and know about.

I am a woman born in the late '20s, who enjoyed higher education in the '40s, was committed to marriage and motherhood in the '50s and '60s, and in part due to the Marty Memorial Scholarship was able to experience a complete change of life style in the '70s and '80s.

My father, born in 1881, was a distinguished academic and my mother, born in 1888, had been awarded an MA from the University of Edinburgh and taught in France before her marriage, not typical accomplishments for women of her generation. However, my parents' marriage was traditional. My mother devoted her energies to supporting my father's career unconditionally by being his social hostess. She was singularly unsuited for the role, being reserved and shy, and with limited physical energy, but she did it well. My father was gregarious, talkative and replenished by apparently inexhaustible sources of energy. This led him to accept many engagements that took him away from home for frequent and lengthy periods of time and my mother was left to cope. Although she had accepted a submissive role, she spoke up when necessary. When I was a student in Grade 12, I was sent home by my home room teacher for wearing slacks to school on the day that we were to decorate the gym for the formal. My mother was furious, and persuaded my father that I should leave a school with such out-of-date teachers. As a result, I spent Grade 13 at Bishop Strachan School where I learned everything I still know about studying, and for the first time experienced a joy in learning from my interaction with a group of eccentric, dedicated women teachers who were superb and tough.

I was a faculty brat. I lived my life from birth to marriage in university housing of one sort or another on campus, as I now do again. My life has come full circle. I suppose that is unusual and I know it has colored all my perceptions of the world.

My parents were both Scots – Orkney Islanders – and both shared the great respect for education that is typical of the Scottish tradition. Their four children – one son and three daughters – were expected to attend school to the highest level possible, to work hard, to do well and to respect their teachers. There was never any suggestion that the expectations were different for young men and women. I did not realize until years later how fortunate I was in this respect. So many of my women friends in adult years told me about the different value placed by their parents on education for sons and daughters and how they had suffered because of this.

Our home was a place where distinguished visitors stayed, and ate with the family in the evening, where conversation was encouraged (unless it involved criticism of teachers or, heaven forbid, sex), where students were entertained, and where I enjoyed a very happy childhood.

I entered Queen's University in 1945, when the class was composed of many recently returned servicemen anxious to get on with their lives and education. I was 16, intellectually curious, naive, and sexually uneducated. My survival without disaster through those years was a triumph of good luck rather than good management. My father had signed the pledge at 18, was still a teetotaler, and no alcohol was served in our house. My introduction to alcohol at university was also a new experience, not always positive for me, or my date!

I was fortunate to be attending a small university with an enrollment of 2,000 students, where most of us knew one another, and where professors were always accessible and often loveably eccentric. The unusual benefit we had as students was that our first-year courses were taught by the best teachers in the university, such as Frank Knox, J.A. Corry, G.B. Harrison, and George Humphrey. It was an exciting time to be at university. Classes were interesting. We felt no anxiety about the future job market, nor the need to obtain high marks to enter graduate school or professional programs. Perhaps because of this, I remember no academic competition between men and women students. However, more important I suspect, few women were really planning to do anything beyond university except marriage, although it was acceptable to go on to Normal School or a job until that desirable state was achieved. I imagine that we therefore were not much of a threat to the men.

98

Elspeth Baugh, Dean of Women, 1983.
CREDIT: Catherine Perkins

Elizabeth and Robert Wallace and Elspeth, 1947

Very few of the women in my class went on to graduate work. Following the family expectation, I did, and enrolled in a graduate program in psychology at the University of Michigan. However, I did the other expected thing and became engaged to a medical student at Queen's before I left for Michigan.

The faculty at Michigan were not pleased with my decision to stay only one year, as they normally did not award Master's degrees. They tried to persuade me that one should continue through to the doctorate to be competent in clinical psychology. I was enjoying my experience at Michigan and was tempted by this proposition. But I remember thinking that there was no real choice for me, as I should get on with the real work of my life, which would be marriage.

I had two significant learning experiences at the University of Michigan that my liberal, intellectual family background and Canadian small-town experience had not provided. The first one was my introduction to sororities, which resulted in my life-long distaste for 'elite' groups of any kind. I was a don in residence at the University, responsible for one hundred first-year women who, like Queen's students, were mostly from small Michigan towns and families with modest incomes. There were, of course, exceptions, and some young women had vast wardrobes, supreme self-confidence and exceptional good looks. Early in the fall, rushing for sororities began and excitement reigned. I was somewhat bemused by this ritual but enjoyed the enthusiasm. I soon became horrified at the end result. When the fatal day came that pledges were offered, I was beseiged by many weeping girls who had not received offers, and were seriously affected by this rejection. Many of these young women were the ones I considered the most worthwhile in terms of character, intelligence and maturity, while some of the more superficial and insensitive girls had received several offers. The whole system was brutal, and operated within a value system that I found repugnant. When I was awakened at night by the beautiful sound of male fraternity brothers singing to a newly 'pinned' young woman, I was not so moved as others around me, although I had to admit it was romantic.

The second learning experience was my first brush with racism. Kingston and Queen's were WASP communities and I had rarely met people of other races and colors; also my parents did not categorize people in those terms. When I arrived at Michigan I joined the Commonwealth Club and there met students from all over the world. I became a good friend of a man from Pakistan who was doing postgraduate work in Law. He was a cultured, gentle and interesting person and I was delighted when he asked me to dinner in Detroit to celebrate my 21st birthday. I was completely unprepared when the black waiter in the restaurant refused to serve us and proceeded to lecture me about my choice of friends. My escort took all this in much better grace than I, undoubtedly because it was not a new experience for him. We retired to a Swedish restaurant, where we were received without comment, and enjoyed a smorgasbord and schnapps, a few gulps of which helped to blot out the earlier experience. I was having my eyes opened to all kinds of discrimination and I did not like what I saw.

In this year at Michigan I also developed an identity as a Canadian. I still had not particularly identified myself as a woman even though I was the only woman in a class of eleven. I did define forever my allegiance to my country in this year. I took in good part the eternal teasing about my pronunciation of out, house and about, but was less amused by being attacked in a meal-line about Canada sending 'only one destroyer' to the Korean war. I found myself for the first time defending my country. I tried not to retort with comment on the late American entry into the Second World War, knowing I would be told they had won the war for us. I am able to sympathize with American students facing anti-Americanism at Queen's from my own experience of being an alien in a foreign land.

When I left Michigan I worked as a clinical psychologist for three years to help put my husband through medical school. It was a happy time. Many of his classmates had married in the same year and all the wives were also working. We became a close social group united by poverty and a common goal, our lives revolving around our husbands' academic program. We were living the traditional life expected of us and I do not think we questioned much of what we were doing. I remember some mild dispute with my husband about housework, as I did it all, and worked a five-and-a-half-day week. He seemed to have time to play golf or sit and listen to music, as well as study, and I felt he might sometimes scrub a floor. His response was that he would do it when he felt it needed doing, and I believe it never got scrubbed again until we moved out of that apartment! I can't remember even thinking that he might help with the meals. I assumed that was my job.

In 1953 our first daughter was born, to our joy, and although I did some part-time work for a few years, I was really a full-time mother for the next fifteen years. We had six children in nine years, all of them wonderful to me, and we lived in Baltimore, Saskatoon and Brockville during this period. My husband had very long hours as a hospital resident, university teacher and finally in a medical practice. I accepted total responsibility for children and household, ignored chronic fatigue and suppressed rage leading to migraines. I found my children fascinating, and I told myself that the rewards in my life usually outweighed the penalties.

Prodded by my husband, I somewhat reluctantly went back to work part-time as a psychologist when my youngest child entered kindergarten. I had been looking forward to some leisure time with all the children in school. However, I soon found that I loved the familiar setting of a child and family clinic, and cheerfully harnessed myself into the double yoke of homemaker and professional, without making any adjustment in my expectations of my responsibilities at home. Nor did anyone else!

My mother called to chide me for neglecting my children. I took my kindergarten child to school on my way to work and picked him up on my way home, hardly neglect, but I did wonder whether mother was right. My son, cleverly sensing that I was feeling some conflict, cried at the school door for weeks and had to be dragged inside by the two kindergarten teachers. I went on to work feeling like an executioner. He later confessed that he was angry at having to leave his best friend, one year younger, who was not yet at school, but I of course had assumed that parting from me was the problem. The same son, with the wisdom of sixteen years, told me when I was wallowing in some form of mother's guilt that I would have to accept that there were other influences in a child's life besides his mother.

What probably stiffened my resolve to continue working was a visit from another doctor's wife who warned me that going to work would kill my social life. I could not have heard better news, as I had always hated the medical socializing and in Brockville had been an unwilling participant in morning sherry parties and very long luncheons. I was the only working wife in that group at the time. I am happy to report that in the medical group in Brockville now there are many professional wives as well as stay-at-home wives, and both life styles seem to be acceptable.

Shortly after I returned to work I investigated the possibility of registration as a psychologist in Ontario. Under the grandfather clause, MA's could be registered; all this legislation had taken place while I was in Saskatchewan and I had heard nothing about it. The registrar of the Board of Examiners told me that my application was two weeks too late. I now had to face the fact that for the rest of my professional life I would only be able to work under the supervision of a registered psychologist, and of course my salary would always be lower than that of a registered psychologist. The only solution to this dilemma was to return to university for a PhD, and that seemed out of the question.

When I returned to work, I began to wish that I could learn more about learning disabilities, and more about school psychology in general. I read what I could find, but wanted more. Finally in 1971, I swallowed my fears and applied to York University for graduate work. I had hoped to be admitted as a part-time student but that option was not available. I began the task of trying to find professors who were still alive who could write references for me, and applied to the Marty Memorial Scholarship. We were by then living in Orillia and, although comfortable, we were far from wealthy. My salary had always been used for family expenses. I felt that I would have to hire a housekeeper to keep things going in the daytime for the children and make the evening meal for the family. I was facing a 70 mile commute twice a day which would mean that I would be away from 6 am to 6 pm. While my husband was supportive, I knew that he would not continue to be if my return to school made a serious drain on our financial resources. Much to my surprise and delight I was admitted to York and won the Marty. I now know that I have Jean Royce, the registrar of Queen's, to thank for the latter. I was the first mature student to be granted the Marty and I believe that Jean with her customary foresight realized this new pattern of education for women would become more common.

I now embarked on a new and exciting venture, although anxious about being a student again. I was so intimidated by the cathedral-like York library that it took me several weeks to learn how to take out a book, and I often felt very out of place in the cafeteria surrounded by youth. My classmates were kind and I made two good women friends in the class, both married but much younger than I. I sometimes faced a horrendous drive through blizzards, but over the years got home every night but two. On those two I was completely snowbound on campus and slept in the psychology lounge, much to the alarm and surprise of the night cleaning staff.

When I look back at my hopeful reports to the Marty committee I marvel at my innocence. What I predicted would take three years ended up taking seven, and, of course, my thesis topic bore no resemblance to the grandiose plan I outlined to them initially.

I am doubly grateful to the Marty. During my first year I began the discouraging search for continuing funding. Many scholarships such as those offered by the IODE and the Ontario Mental Health Association had age limits; usually no one over 35 was eligible. I began to get a message that, at 43, my brain cells should be dead. One male professor also refused to endorse a grant application, arguing it was my husband's responsibility to support me. Therefore I was elated when the Marty committee asked if I would reapply. There were no suitable candidates that year, something that would never happen now when applications have numbered from 40 to 60.

The Marty allowed me to complete my first two residential years. Later I returned to work part-time, then full-time, and was able to pay my own expenses. My years at York were successful only because of significant faculty support. My practicuum supervisor, Dr Malcolm Weinstein, was always there for the hour-a-week supervision, and even allowed me to deposit on his desk tapes which I dictated in the car on my way home. Once he told me that my car's engine was developing an alarming 'ping' which should be attended to. The 'ping' was interfering with the recording. He was so flexible that an hour of supervision might turn into an hour of therapy if that was what I needed, and I often did. My thesis committee serendipitously was composed of three Queen's graduates. They were all supportive, but I remember feeling most comfortable with the two women, who allowed me to blubber on about my difficulties, and sometimes shared their own. I am eternally grateful to the committee member who made me rewrite many more times than I thought reasonable. She was right.

The oral examination was a real crisis. I had become involved in a statistical analysis far beyond my comprehension. I only managed with the help of an amazing woman from the York Institute of Behavioral Studies who had guided me through the unintelligible analysis of my data. I find now, after participating in the oral examinations of several women candidates at Queen's, that I am typical in my feeling that I won this degree by fraud, or because of some sympathetic collusion on the part of the examining committee. Occasionally I look at my thesis, and think it was not great, but better than I thought at the time. Needless to say, I did not attend my graduation.

So far this has been an up-beat story, and has described my gradual evolution from traditional woman to one beginning to see the negative consequences of this traditional role. The day I picked up the first edition of *Ms* magazine in the York bookstore at lunch I became so engrossed that I almost missed my afternoon class. There in print before my eyes was validation of so many ideas I had hardly dared voice to myself, let alone to anyone else. In fact women of my generation usually shared their anger and distress in a form of black humor that had the underlying theme that we were coping, and did not expect change in the way our world was structured. We did not talk to each other honestly.

I cannot say I became a feminist overnight but I travelled a thousand miles that day in my mind, and for the first time began to reflect on the role of women in society and to feel real kinship with other women.

Transitions like this do not occur without a great deal of pain and sometimes loss. During this period both my husband and I had surgery for life-threatening illness. The personal priorities each of us established when close to death were so different that we separated and later divorced. I felt incredible sadness throughout that period, followed by anger. I had to adjust to the new role of single parent on an inadequate income. I found out that telephone and credit card companies do not wish to have a single mother as a customer unless she is willing to submit to an inquisition about her personal and financial affairs. I was told by a police officer that my son, involved in a minor incident, was more suspect because he lived with his mother, instead of in an 'intact' family. I learned a lot of unpleasant things, but also took pride in learning to manage; I had gone directly from my parents' protection to that of my husband, and independence, though scary, was sweet. I now live alone and that, too, took some adjusting to after so many years of family life.

My recognition of myself as a woman emerged slowly. I experienced little discrimination on the basis of gender in my early life, or in my work. Psychologists employed by the Ministry of Health and Community Services in Ontario were always paid on a set scale that was the same for men and women and I found being female an advantage when most of my clients were women and children. The odd father sometimes doubted my word, but the mother usually supported me and we were two against one!

I feel fortunate that I, unlike young women today, was able both to choose to stay home with my children, and to step back into the work force when I was ready. In old age I will see the consequences of so many years of part-time unpensionable work, but I am delighted that many part-time workers are now being given access to pensions. As an unrepentant optimist, I believe that the progress for women's rights, though slow, will continue. I have seen change in my lifetime that I would have not believed possible. I marvel at the reasonably egalitarian marriages of my daughters who share child-care and house work. My sons have not yet married, but they know they can't expect much support from me if they become patriarchs in their marriages. I have been incredibly fortunate, never hungry without food, never sick without care, never alone when I can use Ma Bell to phone one of my children, or one of my friends. I wish all other women could say the same.

Room to grow

PRISCILLA GALLOWAY

I married at nineteen, in 1949, and began teaching in Northern Ontario three years later. Now, within a year, these two foundations of my life have ended. My marriage and career have interwoven themselves through a third of a century; there's no easy separation of the strands; nor is one strand black and the other white; both come in brilliant colours and varying shades of grey.

Why did I need to marry at nineteen, while still in the middle of my undergraduate work at Queen's? The following answers do not make sense in the ambience of the 1980's, but 1949 was a different age, and I was a different person then. First, I felt a need to get committed to one man, to make that decision, before I could get on with my life. Secondly, Bev and I were having sex, which was wicked before marriage. It was not great sex (not surprisingly, considering the environmental problems; nobody had a car at Queen's back then); romantically, I longed for ecstasy; naively, I thought that ecstasy would accompany legitimacy. Further, I was terrified of pregnancy, missing a period more than once, and two periods in a row once, for no other reason than anxiety; I found out later that nausea and tender breasts are my early signals, earlier and surer than lack of blood. Third and perhaps most important, marriage held the illusion of security. My father had his first heart attack at age forty-six during my Grade 13 year; by the time I met Bev family finances were tight. I was Daddy's girl, but Daddy was convinced he had only a short time to live; it was questionable whether he and Mother would ever get out of debt, and my two younger sisters were still in high school. Dad encouraged my marriage, having sized up Bev (quite correctly) as a man with business savvy; the whole thing must have been a relief to him.

Bev had me marked for his own from the time I checkmated him in our first game of chess on our very first date. But what made him special to me? Like most Queen's students in 1948, Bev had been in the armed

Priscilla Galloway, May 1951

forces, the RCAF; he had developed pleurisy 'with effusion, presumed tubercular'; and began his study at Queen's on a veteran's disability allowance. I admired his independence and self-sufficiency; I did not shine in my own eyes by comparison, making no allowance for the differences between age seventeen and twenty-two. I also admired Bev's ability and willingness to express his anger, since I had been brought up in the 'if you can't say something nice, don't say anything at all' school, and had been chilled by the icy silences that were my parents' substitute for angry words.

Above all, I wanted a husband to grow old healthily along with me. Unlike my father, Bev was not an 'all work and no play' man. He was a daily bridge player at the Students' Union, and there was nearly always a weekly poker night with engineering cronies. Saturday afternoon (in season) would see us at the football game, and Saturday evening at the dance at Grant Hall. My own academic load was extra heavy, as I worked to complete an honours degree in English in three intramural years rather than four. Like the wives of his married friends, I edited and typed Bev's essays; I began to fantasize about spending my life with him.

I was still seventeen when we began to date, and had only just turned nineteen when we married in September 1949, at the beginning of my third and Bev's fourth undergraduate year. Taking my two final courses extramurally in Ottawa and in Northern Quebec, I graduated with my class in May of 1951. My first-class honours degree seems a remarkable achievement in the circumstances; our daughter was born in Rouyn-Noranda in October, 1950. Our older son was born eighteen months later.

We paid five thousand dollars for our first house, in Haileybury, with two thousand dollars borrowed from Bev's parents as our down payment. Our first house! It was a two-storey frame house with a huge verandah along the front and one side and an unheated summer kitchen at the back. We spent a happy fall making it beautiful. Bev scraped; I applied eleven and a half gallons of exterior beige, with scarlet trim, keeping an eye on my little ones as best I could.

Then there was the day that I heard a little voice at my feet saying, 'Mummy,' and there was Noël, not yet two years old, on the ladder just below me. She had got up, but could not get down; the ground was twenty feet below. Did I balance the paint can on a window sill or did I simply drop it? 'Hang on, love, Mummy's going to get you.' I had to lean away from the house in order to climb over her; the ground beneath us was sloping the wrong way; for a moment the ladder felt as if it too would sway back and fall away with us near the end of its arc; then I got my position with the child between my body and the rungs, and the ladder settled back against the wall. At that point I knew I could get us down – it was only a matter of taking a few minutes to stop trembling.

The paint job had been finished for only a couple of months when Bev lost his mine geologist's job in nearby Cobalt. We had a three-thousand-dollar mortgage and no savings. My part-time teaching brought in nine dollars a week after paying for childcare. The children and I – like most families of the time – were dependent on our man's ability to earn.

Bev found an exploration job with INCO in the bush of northern Manitoba, hundreds of miles away, and injured his leg there in early spring. Isolated by the spring breakup, he could not get out for six painful weeks while muscles atrophied; restoration of his left leg would take months of intensive therapy. I vaguely recall Bev, on crutches, spending a couple of days with us in Haileybury before continuing to Workmen's (now Workers') Compensation Board hospital near Toronto.

That was a hard time for me too. Walt was about seven months old when Bev left, and Noël an energetic two-year-old. Walt developed infant diarrhoea; my doctor recommended hospitalization, but in those pre-OHIP days we could not afford it. For a month I nursed a sick baby and kept the washing machine in perpetual motion.

I was never warm that winter, and after awhile the cold got to my spirit too. I moved torpidly through mountains of diapers, mountains of coal, mountains of clinkers, mountains of snow. Winter temperatures in Haileybury were often 30 and 40 below zero Fahrenheit. I had no car. I pushed my second-hand seven-dollar baby carriage up and down the steep, snowy roads on book-borrowing and provisioning expeditions and sometimes permitted myself the cop-out of ordering my groceries by phone. The nearest supermarket was five miles away. Food was cheaper there, but I had no way of getting it. Haileybury had no ice delivery, so we had been forced to buy a fridge, but I had no stove until October 1954; I blew the whole of my first month's teaching salary in Toronto on it.

That winter in Haileybury, teaching was my salvation. I taught English to fifty Grade 7 and 8 youngsters in the one classroom on Monday and Thursday afternoons, relieving the Principal, their regular teacher, for administrative duties. On those two afternoons, Mrs Brown came in and looked after my babies and did the ironing, and I had rational converse with thirteen- to fifteen-year-olds. It was wonderful!

I also did supply teaching in both the elementary and secondary schools. Mrs Brown would not come on short notice, and Julie (who would) shocked my neighbours when the beer truck and the boyfriend pulled up at my door. I didn't hear the stories until we were on the verge of leaving town, and wondered how I could have been so obtuse. Julie was a jolly woman, but she was usually particularly jolly when I got home from school.

Children commonly fantasize about the monster in the basement, but I needed no fantasy; the furnace hulked there, drawing coal into its gaping maw, but hoarding the heat in its black iron belly. By day in reality and by night in dreams I shoveled coal and took out clinkers, living in fear that the monster would go out and I would be unable to start it again.

Spring came at last.

Bev and I decided to move to Toronto, since Bev was to be there for months of therapy. My early dreams of going into journalism or working for the United Nations were finally abandoned. I liked teaching and wanted the security of my teaching certificate; the training could be obtained only in Toronto.

I sold the Haileybury house and put our furniture in storage. We rented a housekeeping room on Ward's Island, in Toronto harbour, from which I made forays by ferry, always with the children, to look at houses to buy. In August we bought the house in which we would live for the next twelve years.

At age twenty-two, I had spent the best part of a year alone with two small children, working part-time, had sold a house and managed a major move. I did not set out to do all this; one event led to another; but it was good to know some of my own strength.

In September I contracted hepatitis, but managed to ignore the nausea and dizziness while completing registration at the Ontario College of Education; then I spent six weeks in hospital. In order to stay in the teacher training course, I signed myself out, against medical advice, for the first practice teaching week.

I was one of only three married women with children at OCE in 1953-4 and the only one with pre-schoolers. Daycare was not a word in the language of the time; mothers of small children were supposed to be at home. The childcare arrangements I had made barely survived my hospital stay; as he took me home on Saturday, Bev told me that we would somehow have to find care for the children effective the following Monday. Through a newspaper ad, we found a woman to take them in her home. The next week we hired the first of half a dozen live-in housekeepers. We rented out the upstairs of our storey-and-a-half house; our family had the two main-floor bedrooms. The housekeeper shared one with the children; Bev and I had the other.

Unlike most trainees, I remember OCE fondly, exulting in even a quasi-intellectual atmosphere again after three-and-a-half years in the wilderness of small mining towns where I knew nobody and was not free to get to know anybody much. I loved my babies, but their care was exceedingly restricting, and I was still very young.

As the year progressed, the prospect of a teaching career became more and more attractive. I could certainly have got a job outside the Toronto area, but after his hospital stay Bev had apprenticed with a Toronto firm of land surveyors, and we had bought a house. The Toronto area was my job market, but beginning teachers usually did not find places there. As a competitor, I had three strikes against me: marriage, youth and children.

Betty Friedan was later to document brilliantly the effect on American women of the social messages sent to them at the end of WWII: go back home where you belong; leave the paid jobs to the men. Those messages were part of the social structure I experienced in 1954. It's not easy to act in contradiction to such messages. If Bev had not lost his job, if he had not been injured, if I had not been reminded so forcibly that there was no necessary security in husband or father, I too might have been a frustrated Friedan housewife, at least while the children were small. Although divine intervention was not immediately apparent, the Goddess must have had me in Her hands.

In 1954, the Borough of York still required a woman teacher to resign on marriage, although the other Toronto area Boards were more broadminded. North York was where I wanted to teach, since that was where we had bought our house. North York, however, refused to interview me for the one appropriate position, turning me down flat in less than a minute on the telephone. My first-class Honours degree in English and my straight-A record in practice teaching were irrelevant; I had two pre-school children. Although one of the ablest trainees, I was the last in my class of twelve English teachers to get a job, and was left in no doubt that I was lucky to be teaching English at $2800 per year at Malvern Collegiate in Toronto in September 1954. North York was quick enough to hire me in 1956, when its growth spurt was beginning. By then I could wave a permanent English Specialist's Certificate and point to two years of teaching without one day of absence.

Glenn, my third child, was born in 1958. There was no maternity leave, and I had to resign, but had no trouble getting rehired a year and a half later. The last four months of my pregnancy was a halcyon time. My day began with a natural childbirth class at Mothercraft, and continued at a carrel at the University of Toronto library where I worked on my MA thesis, a study of the symbolism of Tennyson's 'Palace of Art.' I had kept Nan, who had by then been our housekeeper for five years; the household organization was intact. Bev and his survey crews were working on one hundred and twenty-five miles of legal survey for Trans-Canada Pipe Lines between Long Lac and Hearst. I was glad to see him on the brief occasions when he got home; meanwhile, the low-key, low-stress life was a luxury, and I wallowed contentedly in it. The next year was much busier. I did not teach, but did not have the leisure for my baby that had been my plan, being busy managing, renovating and re-renting a twenty-eight-suite apartment building. It was a challenge which I met successfully, but I was pleased to hand the building over to Bev and return to teaching in September 1959.

For eleven years, I taught English in three different high schools and was assistant head for four of those years. There was no opportunity for me to apply for the first assistant headship available. My Principal explained that the school valued my ability, but was giving the position to a man who had a wife and children to support. It seemed ironic, because my husband was still on apprenticeship wages, and I was the main support of my family. However, I thought it was decent of the principal to tell me that I'd been in the running. A couple of years later, the assistant headship was mine.

Highlighting my nine years at Northview was my work in designing and teaching English courses for bright students, beginning with a post-Sputnik experiment in acceleration and continuing with enrichment courses in Grades 10 and 12. I kept my original superb students for all three years, experimenting with the program and training the teachers who followed me. Every now and again I hear good things about one or another of those young people and rejoice; every now and again, a little credit for what they have been able to do comes my way. I seem to have been more sure of myself in those days. Ah, youth!

In those years, I was completing my MA at U of T in English, and beginning to work with professional associations of English teachers. Northrop Frye was delivering the lectures that were my introduction to current Canadian literature. When Margaret Laurence burst upon the literary scene in 1964, I had six copies of *The Stone Angel* and *The Tomorrow Tamer* circulating in my special Grade 12 class within a month of publication. Those were heady days.

My second and most important promotion came in 1968: Language Arts Consultant. At thirty-eight, I was the youngest of three women reporting to a much younger man. Our English coordinator in North

York, however, was a woman; under her leadership, our English Department did landmark work. I was particularly involved in linguistics and secondary school reading. Back to grad school I went, this time to the Ontario Institute for Studies in Education, for training to help me as a change agent in schools. At the same time, I laid out a plan to qualify as a doctoral candidate.

Bev had long since stopped speaking of teaching as my hobby. He did not read fiction or poetry, although we enjoyed theatrical comedies and ballet together. He was pleased that some recognition was coming my way, although to him I seemed over-involved in my work. After more than twenty years of a professional salary and frugal living, I should reasonably have been able to finance my return to doctoral studies out of savings, but in fact I had none in 1975, not even a bank account in my own name. We had fallen into the pattern of having joint accounts. All savings, all excess funds of every variety and many a dollar that was not excess at all, went into the business which was called 'ours,' but which was controlled by Bev. For more than twenty years, in addition to my teaching career, I did all the office work for the business, everything except answer the phone during the day; in the summer I did that too. For more than ten years in the late 1950s and early 1960s there were always ten or eleven men on the payroll; in the summers twenty to thirty. I ran white prints by the score on our small German machine. Our office was the upstairs of our storey-and-a-half home; there was a separate entrance but only one telephone line; there was no separation between the business and our personal lives.

At one time and another, I ran other businesses 'for us,' notably the apartment building and a trailer park and tent campsite. We began the park; Bev originally planned to sell it after one year, but he never found the right buyer; I insisted that it be sold the year I finally got my big promotion; by that time I had been running it for five years.

In 1976, in my PhD study, I should have been able to draw on the business for my needs; I never drew any salary for all this work. However, Bev felt personally threatened by my study. The sexist picture that I uncovered was shocking. I alternated between rage and depression. It would have been splendid if my husband had been able to share my feelings, but it was hardly surprising, given his own conditioning, that he could not. We continued to share living quarters but virtually stopped speaking to each other.

I worked on a wooden worktop suspended on two two-drawer files, in a small upstairs room filled, walls and centre, with wooden bookcases. I had stained shelves and spindles from kits and put the bookcases together myself; the nutmeg coloured wood was warm and friendly, but I was totally encased in the materials of my study, and felt claustrophobic and alone.

Later, the analysis was complete and the major task was writing up the results. In the strained atmosphere of the house, however, writing was difficult. At one point I reserved a room in one of the York University residences and packed a suitcase. By the time the suitcase was closed, however, I was trembling violently; it was only too obvious that I could not, even temporarily, move out and continue to function. Earlier, I had tried to negotiate to get a room downtown and work during the week at Robarts, where I had a carrel, coming home on weekends; Bev had totally opposed this plan, putting the marriage on the line, and I had given in.

Queen's women supported my second year of doctoral study with the Marty Scholarship in 1976-7. I had no way of knowing it at the time, but in retrospect there is no doubt: I could not have completed my study without that support. The award gave me room to grow.

The Marty money paid my dissertation expenses: much of the traveling to collect data; all of the costs of typing, reproducing and binding; and a large part of the cost of books. I had to buy a lot of books. The U of T Robarts Library did not number among its four million titles the new books of feminist literary research needed as background reading for my study of 'Sexism and the Senior English Literature Curriculum in Ontario Secondary Schools.' School literature textbooks have not been collected anywhere; I had to gather my own collection of more than four hundred titles.

I knew when I received the Marty Award how much I valued the honour, and what a relief it was to have four thousand five hundred dollars in my control. I know now that my dissertation and my later book, *What's wrong with high school English? ... It's sexist, unCanadian, outdated*, owe their existence to that support from the women of Queen's.

Bev gave some financial support in my Marty year, diverting two hundred and twenty dollars per month to me. He felt that this was generous; neither of us realized how much more would be needed. Neither of us was being very rational with the other. I was stretched far beyond what I had ever thought my limits might be; more than anything else, I remember being rather surprised and pleased that I continued to produce good work.

When the date of October 17 was set for my dissertation oral, I did not tell Bev; it would have added to an almost intolerable stress. He raged, convinced that the study would never be done. I wasn't sure myself. I moved to the cottage in July 1977 and wrote there overlooking Georgian

Bay. When I started back to work for North York in September, after two years' leave, the work was essentially complete.

My writing career had begun with adult short stories and poetry in 1974; a few of my short stories and some poetry have appeared in Canadian literary magazines; two major sales of short stories, one to *Chatelaine* and one to the CBC, were the biggest thrills of my life in the late 1970s. Like many men married to women writers, Bev had great difficulty with the whole idea. A very private person, he found the notion of baring one's feelings in public abhorrent, and the idea that any version of him might be encapsulated (through my perspective) in a story was absolute anathema. His extreme reaction was no doubt partly why I began writing for children. A confirmed literary junky, I love being part of the Canadian literary scene.

Good Times, Bad Times, Mummy and Me was published in 1980, within a month of the book based on my PhD research, *What's wrong with high school English? ... It's sexist, unCanadian, outdated*. My prose anthology *Timely and Timeless* followed, along with picture books *When You Were Little and I Was Big*, and *Jennifer Has Two Daddies*. It's very exacting, writing picture books; one has so few words in which to tell the story that each word becomes much more important than in, for instance, an adult novel. Writing is the most absorbing and engrossing activity of my life.

Ambitions alter according to circumstance. For years I had wanted to live and work in New Zealand, my mother's homeland; and so in August 1985 I set out for a year's exchange as a lecturer at Teachers' College in Christchurch, the city where my mother was born.

I left Canada with my family's messages of love displayed in brilliant magic marker on the plaster cast encasing my broken left leg. Bev, who had earlier felt betrayed and abandoned by my plans, came to understand my longing to experience my maternal heritage, and to do it while my two aunts, now eighty-nine and eighty-three, were still alive. He ran my errands and chauffeured me as needed, even cording the taped Pampers box inside which my Macintosh word processor nestled, cushioned by my scuba wetsuit.

Bev took me, two enormous suitcases, and the Pampers box to the airport at 9 am on August 7, 1985. We had by then been living separately for more than five years, but our lives continued to be intertwined; hard not to be, after thirty-six years. Perhaps if I had needed to force a property settlement, our relationship really would have ended; as it was, I had after my doctorate taken control of my own salary, and was comfortable in an

Priscilla Galloway and friends at Bishopdale School, Christchurch, New Zealand, February 1986. CREDIT: Derek Tonkin.

apartment. After growing very far apart, we were cautiously enjoying each other's company. He was to join me in New Zealand in December for my summer holiday.

Our parting at the airport was flurried; with my cast and cane, a wheelchair was needed, and the flight attendant was waiting. Bev never was any good at displaying emotion in public; he bent awkwardly to brush my cheek, but there were tears in both our eyes as I was wheeled away.

Less than three months later he was dead.

I was loving my work at college and my relatives, and had even managed one excellent day of scuba. After seventeen years as a resource person working with teachers and students in many schools, I was rediscovering the pleasures of being part of a large and interesting staff. As a high school teacher I never spent much time in the staff room, but at college I discovered that much business gets done over morning and afternoon tea, in addition to some pleasant relaxation and socializing. Leisure – any sustained feeling of leisure – has been outside my experience; I began to discover that I too could take time to savour my life.

Euphoria was shattered by death. Instead of introducing Bev to my New Zealand relatives and touring the South Island with him, I flew home for his funeral. Instead of scuba in Australia and the Solomons, I spent my summer vacation in Ontario snow, beginning to sort out the complex mess that may follow a totally unexpected death. Bev was an old-style entrepreneur; romance for him involved little deals here and there; filing was not his forte, but I think he had kept every piece of paper that had come into the house since we bought it in 1964; five years' worth of receipts for accounts paid by cheque were piled haphazardly on top of one of the filing cabinets.

Bev died peacefully in his sleep, but no cause of death was apparent; in fact, exhaustive tests by the coroner's office over the following five months failed to reveal a cause. During this whole time, my children and their families and I reached out for each other. The Christmas season was a round of family events at all our different homes, made all the more precious by the fact that soon my 'summer holiday' would end. I left for New Zealand again on January 15, 1986.

Perhaps I shall one day manage a less frenetic life, though events seem to conspire against me. Within a month, the Ontario government amended the Teachers' Superannuation Act; I could retire at the end of August 1986 on a years-of-service pension. Nineteen eighty-six is the first September since 1958 that I have not been starting back to school; there have been only three such Septembers since I began kindergarten at five years old.

We've always been a busy and productive family, I and mine, and now we are learning to work together in our family affairs. The skills of an MBA business executive, a real estate salesperson, and a teacher/musician supplement each other very well indeed. At times we wish Bev's expertise were available to us, but our affairs are, on the whole, working out surprisingly well. If any of Bev's quite unusual energy survives, I'm confident it would be directed towards helping us; perhaps it is. I don't dismiss such a possibility out of hand as I would have done twenty years ago.

At times over the past thirty years, I've felt I had it all, all the things the women's movement has worked for, a good professional career and recognition, in addition to marriage and children. At other times, it seems that my career has been very much limited by my sex, and that Bev's domination extended over every aspect of our home. I've had my share of hard times, and would like to believe that those times are past. I have (unlike many women of my time) a good professional pension. I have a house, not just a room of my own, and intend to indulge in creative renovation to build a marvelous workspace for my writing self.

It seems important to write this record, not in bitterness, but as a matter of fact, to say, this is how it was for me and, in essence, for many other women of my time. I was oppressed, but we were well taught to acquiesce in our own oppression. Many women today have never felt themselves to be oppressed and so believe that oppression of women, in Canada at least, is past. It is lessened, but not past, and much of it has gone underground. No principal today would tell a female applicant for an English headship that he believed no female could handle the job, although that was the response I got to my first application. The fact that it would no longer be stated, however, does not mean that it is no longer felt.

A week ago I bought a sailboard, on which I am beginning to get my balance. I hope that learning to use it is a bit like learning to ride a bicycle; you keep falling off and falling off and then suddenly you're on to it. Maybe life is like that.

Learning from women's history

LIN MORENCY BUCKLAND

Answering the question 'Where are you from?' is not a straightforward matter for me, so I've taken to replying with a twist on the phrase that's used to describe the Canadian national identity, saying that my variegated roots are 'multicultural within a bilingual framework.'

I was born in Montreal to a French-Canadian mother and a father whose family had immigrated from England around 1910. I'm not sure to what extent my parents' marriage was representative of the overcoming of the two solitudes by young Canadian people in the 1940's, but I remember that in my early years the two families intermingled on special occasions with warmth, music, and much cross-cultural teasing that must have harkened back to the more serious rivalries that they had experienced on the streets of working class neighbourhoods in Montreal.

When I was still very young my parents emigrated to the United States. My misty images of those years in a small New England town resemble a Norman Rockwell painting. We lived in an old house that my parents devotedly restored. My father worked at his office all day, while my mother stayed home and looked after me and my newly arrived sister. My main memory of this period is that there was inevitably a severe snowstorm at the time of my February birthday, so my birthday parties were always having to be cancelled – a situation that was rectified rather dramatically by our next move.

When I was about nine, my parents decided to move to a warmer and more humid climate to relieve my father's severe asthma. My mother's china was carefully packed in specially built barrels; we left behind our winter coats and blankets, and set sail on a ship for Jamaica, where my father and an uncle went into business together.

I never realized that there was something special in this willingness of my parents to uproot and begin completely new life experiences elsewhere. Now, when people hear about my background, they often express

Morency family portrait. From left to right, Irene Morency (maternal grandmother); Pauline Morency (mother); Lorraine Porter (sister); Lin Buckland; Jeannine Morency (aunt); Laura Buckland (daughter) in front.

amazement when they compare their own sedate upbringing in the same town, often in the same house, with my family's energetic traipsings. But I have valued the experience: certainly, moving and travelling inculcate by necessity an openness to different kinds of people, food, music, and perspectives. You learn also to focus on the quality friendships that will endure through long-distance nurturing, for it seems that people who travel extensively or live in different countries are naturally attracted to others who also do the same, which carries the bonus of widening your knowledge and appreciation of different cultures even more.

North Americans tend to think of West Indians in literal black and white terms. It is true that the large majority of Jamaican people are black and that for many years the tiny colonial elite was white. However, the Jamaican population, and particularly the middle class, includes the descendents and mixtures of descendents of many nationalities and ethnic groups; the Jamaican motto is actually 'Out of many one people.' My years in Jamaica therefore added on to my French-Canadian, British, and New England base a whole range of new cultural exposures, all melded and filtered through the unique culture that comes of the Jamaican experience. At boarding school, the group of us who shared a dormitory, the stresses and antics of high school years, and close teenage friendships, included Chinese, Syrian, African, Spanish, East Indian, and South American, as well as North American elements in our backgrounds. Our midnight feasts were particularly memorable, as we pooled 'tuck,' brought back from each of our raids during holidays on distinctive family larders.

I've often wondered if this multicultural, multisocial background explains why my academic history has been characterized by interdisciplinary and multidisciplinary interests. While I describe myself now as an historical sociologist, or a sociological historian, my intellectual interests and experiences have led me along a number of disciplinary paths, including literature, philosophy, economics, and educational theory.

In correspondence during the early stages of the project to create this book, one Marty Scholar referred to 'the gentle fostering world of women' when she discussed the role that the Marty and the University Women's Scholarship had played in her career. I would highlight the influence of women in my intellectual development as well, the most obvious example being that my primary and secondary education was received in an all-female environment.

In my life, however, the beacons of strength in pursuing goals, enthusiasm in exploring new ideas, sharpness in critical perspective, and a healthy ability to see the humourous side of experiences, were not only set up for me by women teachers but also by my female relatives.

My maternal grandmother married when she was 17, and had five children by age 24, at which time her husband left her. Faced with the responsibility of supporting five children, she borrowed $50.00 from her parents, took a hairdressing course, and set up her little shop in the front room. She worked six days a week at her business, and then spent Sundays travelling on streetcars from one end of the city to the other, visiting her children and picking up and delivering their laundry at the religious charitable institutions where they were being cared for. Operating a small personal services business in a French working class district of Montreal was by no means a route to wealth, but my grandmother did manage to successfully support and raise her family alone – ironically in a social and religious context in which the idea of a separated, single parent independent business woman was inconceivable.

On my father's side, I had two aunts who have always been linked together in family lore, even though they had each spent about 30 years of their lives married. Neither of them had any children, and they had both worked since they were very young for the Bell Telephone. After retirement, they spent their final active 20 or so years travelling the globe together, returning home to the apartments which they had each taken in the same building following their respective widowhoods.

My aunts had collectively spent over 80 years in the paid labour force. When I began to research women's history, they were enthused (and quite amused), responding to my questions about what it had been like to work as telephone operators in the early days. They told me about some of the rules and regulations that characterized the 'production line' of operators: they would have to line up to enter their shift, could only take washroom breaks at certain times, weren't allowed to talk or eat on the job, and were under strict supervision as they carried out work that was often stressful (and physically dangerous in the case of electrical shocks). Yet in the same breath as their fairly clear-eyed critical perceptions about their working lives, my aunts would express pride in their contribution to the development of the sector and obviously took pleasure in their status as Bell 'Pioneers'.

This capacity of women to pull a sense of pride and dignity out of experiences which they also recognize to be unjust is one of the strongest themes that I have carried from my relationship with my own female relatives and seen reflected in my research in women's history.

Perhaps initially at least, my own mother's early and middle adult years seem to conform to the typical image of the 1950's woman. She worked as a clerk (also for the Bell Telephone) until her marriage, contributing right on cue to the post world war baby boom (I was born in 1947), and devoting her years after that to the unpaid work of running a household and raising children. Yet, like all my grandmother's children, she is a highly articulate, intellectually intense, artistically sensitive, and critically aware person. She is largely self-educated. I am amazed when I remember the books that she eagerly encouraged me to read at age 13. At that point, of course, romantic novels (especially trashy ones) were more appealing to my adolescent taste than Julian Huxley, Simone de Beauvoir, and Bertrand Russell, but several years later when I embarked on my own intellectual searches, I knew which works to turn to, because my mother had already shown me the route.

Now at 64, my mother would likely encourage me to take up back-packing, or to travel the Arctic, or to build a hand-hewn house, all avenues which she is enthusiastically exploring while also adjusting to being in the paid labour force herself after a 40 year absence. Obviously, if my mother continues to serve as a role model, I must anticipate a period of hyperactivity once I hit 60.

When I won the Marty, I assumed that it was some strange anomaly. Somehow, despite the confirmed acceptability of my work, I didn't think that I was a real scholar, because my own life seemed to be so far removed from what I imagined was the smooth process through which academics serenely passed: straight from high school to the university of your choice; living in residence and attending football rallies wearing your school colours; taking some time for travel in Europe; then graduate school, a solid MA thesis (in one discipline) leading neatly and logically to the PhD dissertation topic; publications building on this clearly defined area of expertise; a tenure track position, and a most agreeable life happily ever after.

In contrast to this vision, my undergraduate degree was pursued at four universities in three provinces, after I had spent several years working as a clerk-secretary, had married, and had had two children. I spent half my time as an undergraduate typing my way through the tuition fees and children's day care costs; I spent most of my MA trying to master the basis of several different disciplines. Then, just when I discovered that my true professional calling in life was to lecture and do research, the bottom fell out of the academic job market. My PhD has been interrupted twice; I now earn my living as a bureaucrat; and the publications that I've managed to produce over the past few years have little direct application to my scholarly interests.

Yet the interesting thing is that the 'square-pegness' of this saga is not really all that atypical for many women in the academic world (or with aspirations to be). In fact, when I served as a member of the Marty Selection Committee a few years ago, I saw that there were many women doing Marty-calibre academic work and proposing projects of outstanding scholarly merit from a basis of life circumstances and experiences that were anything but typical of the image. While institutions might be taking some time to officially recognize and accommodate these realities, growing numbers of women are returning to school.

In my own case my sister and I had grown up with the expectation that we would attend university, but, when I graduated from high school and returned to Canada, a turn of family circumstances made it impossible at that time. So I went out into the work force (at what I consider to be a shockingly young age now that I have teenaged children of my own). I started off working as a file clerk for an insurance company, but because I had a high school certificate – and could type – I moved relatively quickly up the ladder through clerical jobs in another insurance company, a trust company, and Bell Telephone (obviously following in the family footsteps!) until I finally landed a fairly interesting job as secretary/receptionist for the executive of a small Scandinavian import firm. I took pride in my work; I know that like most secretaries I brought intelligence, thought and initiative to my job, and, like most secretaries, I was paid an appallingly low amount of money for doing so.

I married (also at what I consider to be a shockingly young age now that I have teenaged children of my own); and several years later my husband was transferred to Newfoundland, and we began our family. I worked at home for a period of time, looking after my two young babies, but before the youngest was a year old I had started a night course in English literature at Memorial University. The following year, I took two literature courses, one at night and one during the day while the children went to play nursery. I had the idea at the time that I would simply take hundreds of literature courses. I couldn't see the point of a degree, but being able to read, savour, analyse and write about my books was a dramatic and welcome contrast to my other world of diapers, apple juice, and baking wholewheat cookies.

In my second year in Newfoundland, the feminist activist Bonnie Krepps came to give a public lecture. When she spoke on women's liberation and showed film clips of Ti Grace Atkinson and Kate Millett giving speeches,

126

I didn't relate it very easily to my diapers, and apple juice, but those early teenaged readings of Simone de Beauvoir encouraged by my mother seemed to have created a receptive base. When the local health food store carried notice of a forming women's group, I signed up.

As an active feminist now, I wish I could present being a member of the first Consciousness Raising group in St John's, Newfoundland, as some kind of gold-plated credential, but in fact the experience wasn't like that at all. Most of the other women were graduate students or junior (what else?) lecturers and if I didn't feel entirely intimidated I sensed that they had more manouevering room than I. With two young babies to feed, and memories of that appallingly low salary as a secretary, I was hardly able to contemplate delivering an ultimatum about my rights to my husband.

And yet, I continued to feel a part of something larger. In my own, not-very-well-informed way, and with varying degrees of cooperation and resistance from my husband, I tried to live non-stereotyped roles and practise non-sexist child rearing. I paid attention to the connection between toys, games, clothes, and assumptions; I continually pointed out the sex role stereotyping in books, on television, and, much to their embarrassment, in the birthday gifts of Barbie dolls and trucks imposed on my children by their friends. (They still tease me about overloading them with stuffed animals.) I tried to encourage my boy and my girl to each develop both gentleness and strength. And in my literature courses – I started choosing to write critical essays from my perspective as a woman.

Now I believe that it is these types of undocumented, unpublicized, and unanalysed efforts by women that represent major and powerful contribution to social change.

By the time we moved to Kingston, Ontario, I had decided that I wanted to pursue a university degree. This was a major undertaking, financially and logistically. Obviously, we needed good child-care, but when we applied to the municipal child care centre I was told, 'You don't have to go to university, you could just stay home and look after them yourself.' In order to pay for the children's care in a private centre, and to cover the costs of tuition fees, books, etc., I took a part-time job on campus, working as a secretary each afternoon. This complicated my available time for classes and hence my course selection, which was already constrained by such considerations as not taking courses during the children's supper and bedtime hour. My studying had to be done in the quiet hours of the night when the family was asleep, and since my daytime hours on campus were filled to saturation by classes, my job, and required hours for the cooperative day care, situations such as required readings that were on 'library-only' reserve created extra stresses.

However, at Queen's I found humane and sensitive people in the administration who took the time to help me through the hundreds of hoops. This support ranged from people in the Student Awards Office helping me apply for independent assessment for a Canada Student Loan (the forms and procedures could only accommodate me if I presented myself as a dependent of my husband each time it referred to 'parents'), to professors sympathetically understanding my frozen feet at the prospect of writing exams after years out of school. The Padre's office helped arrange an emergency bursary when the strain of sudden school-related expenses put additional strains on the marriage, and the student outreach that operated from the VP's office at the time gave me cups of coffee and pep talks about the intrinsic value of education on the frequent occasions when I found myself questioning whether all the effort was worth it.

Much to my delight, once in graduate school at the Institute of Canadian Studies, Carleton University, I began to win substantial scholarships, and the effect of being relieved of the financial necessity to type showed immediately in my work, which in turn led to more scholarships and Teaching Assistantships. I threw myself into graduate studies with what can only be described as passion; I found the experience of learning, exploring, and integrating new ideas into my undergraduate knowledge base so heady that I even took more courses than were required for my program. I went with interdisciplinary zeal from seminars on Canadian history in the morning to lectures on social stratification theory in the afternoon. I got so absorbed in my research that I would forget when it was my turn to car pool the children from nursery school.

As a teaching assistant, I found that I loved being able to interact with a group of undergraduates. I was offered increasingly interesting TAships, and eventually the opportunity of a sessional lectureship in the Canadian Society course that had first fired my sociological imagination. This course was offered at night during the summer, and I found it so stimulating and fulfilling to teach (and learn from) other adults, that I applied and was hired the following fall to lecture in sociology to continuing education students at Algonquin College.

I continued as a part-time sessional lecturer at both Algonquin College and Carleton University, but once the tenure of my scholarships was over I was faced with the fact that the income from this work was not sufficient to meet my financial responsibilities, especially now that I was a single parent. I began taking temporary clerical jobs to 'support my teaching habit.'

In this experience, I was typical of the many women who are working in the marginalized sectors of the academic world. Sessional lecturers are often asked to teach new courses at the last minute, and, for love of teaching and the desire to continue gaining relevant experience, they take the task on. But it means that sessionals are often almost continuously involved in developing new courses, ironically when they often don't have the luxury of time or the same level of institutional support as tenured faculty. Moreover, under some contracts, sessionals are only paid for classroom hours; this means that all the course development, preparation of lectures, development of reading lists, assignments, and all of the marking gets done on a volunteer basis. Combined with the need to take on several jobs (either in the academic context or outside of it), this whole situation results in almost no remaining time or energy for research, writing, and publications – and hence for professional development and competitiveness for an academic career.

When the juggling of sessional lectureships and clerical contracts began to wear me down, and I recognized that the prospects of breaking that cycle were low, I went to the Canada Manpower Centre and asked if I could be re-trained in some field that was in demand in the job market. I can now tell this story with a fine sense of the irony of a would-be academic working as the operator of a processor of words, but at the time I was absolutely devastated at the suggestion that after all my years of study I should be typing again. I decided to move to Toronto for the wider job market there.

While organizing my family and effects for the move, I learned that I had won a Social Sciences and Humanities Research Council fellowship to commence a PhD. I decided that I would take the doctorate at the Ontario Institute for Studies in Education, University of Toronto (OISE). There, I could take courses in adult education and higher education policy, which, given certain demographic and economic trends, seemed to be areas where public policy and planning bodies would require expertise. And at the same time, at OISE I could also focus on the history of women and education, and thus keep my own academic research interests active.

My time at OISE was productive, and it was especially stimulating to work in a context of active feminist scholarship, but it was a challenge to survive as a single parent family on an SSHRC in Toronto. Under those circumstances a fridge breaking down can spell disaster. After several such catastrophes, I regretfully declined my second year SSHRC and went out on the job market again.

My hunches about the kind of specializations that might be needed in the labour market turned out to be good ones, and I obtained a series of contracts and then eventually a full-time job with the provincial government. I continued to study part-time, but ironically, while much of my policy research has focussed on accessibility for adult students, particularly women, university policy prevented my own part-time courses from being counted towards my doctorate.

Interestingly enough, during the same period that my life circumstances were leading me away from the academic world, I moved more deeply into women's history. In particular, I had an accumulated influence of my own 'foremothers,' as well as the recent inspiration of the strong feminist scholars with whom I had worked at OISE.

When a friend from a women's history collective moved to Toronto, she and I found ourselves discussing the insights we had gained from oral history research. We were particularly fascinated by what we had learned about women's role in the economic development of the North, for while it seems obvious that all the men who laboured in logging, mining and railway building also needed food, accommodation, laundry, and other daily maintenance services, women's work in providing these services has tended to be left out of formal accounts of economic history.

Our taped interviews with elderly women in Northern Ontario contained dramatic and moving accounts of how they had contended, often as newly arrived immigrants, with the physical and emotional demands of pioneering and community building in a harsh environment. The many women who ran boarding houses, for example, told us of rising at 5 am to bake 10 loaves of bread and 18 pies, before preparing breakfasts and lunches for 20 men, while simultaneously caring for their children. One woman told us that every time she uses the automatic washing machine now, she remembers the years of trying to get the coal dust out of workmen's clothes, which were laundered in big cauldrons of water heated on the wood stove, for, of course, all of these tasks had to be done without the benefit of electricity or running water. And yet, once again, the strongest theme that came from the women's own accounts of their years of hard work was a sense of pride and accomplishment.

As we listened, and re-listened to the taped interviews, our growing respect for these women heightened our determination to share their stories more widely. We embarked on the development and presentation of a multi-media program that eventually included not only excerpts of the taped voices of women telling their own stories, but the projection of historical photographs, a narrated script giving the historical background of women's work in the 1900-1930 period, and dramatic interpretations of some stories by a professional actor.

Carrying out all the technical, creative, and coordination tasks of this project when we both had full-time jobs and demanding personal lives was a story in itself, but if some day some young whippersnapper feminist historians came along and asked us to talk about the time we did the community history project, I know I would certainly remember it as one of my most satisfying experiences.

So where has all this history led me?

I now earn my living as a public servant, with the official-sounding title of 'policy analyst.' Essentially, my job consists of doing research, analysis, synthesis, and writing, usually under deadlines that would put an academic into shock; of course, in contrast to the academic world, I do this work on subjects not of my own choosing. In spite of this, I enjoy my job. I am genuinely interested in public policy, and appreciate that skills such as analysis and writing can never be practised too often. I also gain satisfaction out of using my expertise as a community volunteer on women's issues and adult education.

This year, for the first time after a long gap, it is finally possible to spend some time and energy on my own research. I am doing reading courses on a topic expanded from my earlier doctoral research, around the history of women's work in the service sector. My routine is to try to devote one out of every seven days to studying, and there are frequently whole months when other demands make that impossible. But I am quite happy proceeding this way for a period of time, hoping in a few years to arrange leave and complete the PhD.

I look towards the future with interest and optimism. My children will be out on their own in a few years; my life will take on a different shape. Perhaps I will journey to visit my mother, who will presumably be in the Arctic – or Africa. I find that my multicultural roots are asserting themselves; more and more I want to spend time working, studying, and living in different intellectual and social contexts. Then after all that, I shall come home to Canada to live by the sea, and write stories about women's history.

The happy vessel

Judith Thompson

When I first applied for a Marty Fellowship, I was in dire straits. My first play, *The Crackwalker*, had been produced on a tiny stage in a theatre that seated about sixty people. Most nights about thirty people showed up. I would stand outside on the street, willing any approaching person to buy a ticket. Mostly, they were going past the theatre. Opening night was an experience unlike any other in my life. It was not a glamorous occasion, but I felt these characters, that sprang to life through me and the actors, connect with an audience. This was a ferocious spark, like thunder – emotions usually kept buried deep were bubbling and surfacing in many of the audience members – in some cases, such as the *Globe and Mail*'s Norma Harrs, the emotion was vitriol! In others it was, I guess, horror and pity, the old Aristotelian twosome. I was sky high; all the months of strange eye twitches, huge boils, crying sessions were worth it. This was an event. I remember the clear November night. We walked the few miles home after the party. The next morning still high, hung over, my husband Gregor ran out to get a paper. We opened it excitedly, assured by the standing ovation that the notice would be good. We saw the headline ... and couldn't believe our eyes. This couldn't be right. Did she see what we saw? Of course I have blocked that headline out of my mind. We both said 'oh no.' Just 'oh no.' Then we got the *Sun*. It was, of course, even worse. I cried and cried like a baby on the bed. The opinion of two people, as individuals, is not very important to me, but when it is in print! – it's as if a child is in the middle of a huge circle of taunting, spitting enemies, and one reacts like a child .... Anyway, despite the press, the word of mouth was very good, and with each subsequent production got better.

However, a *success d'estime* does not mean money. I landed a rather shameful job doctoring a screenplay. I didn't realize till I started working on it that it had been soft-porn – an accountant's write off ... And of

Judith Thompson
CREDIT: Michael Cooper

course I unwittingly broke union rules by working for this sleazy, non-union outfit. In the end, nobody but me got paid at all.

That year, my husband took a year off between his second honours BA and his MA to work at a construction job, making a pittance. We suddenly realized that my success did not mean money. I also knew for certain that, being an extremely nervous person, ordinary jobs like waitressing left me so psychologically exhausted that I would not have anything left to write plays. And writing a play is not something that can be done in a few spare hours. It takes, for me, years of thought, a year or so of putting images together, and then at least a solid year of writing and re-writing and re-writing. Then I might have a play. Of course I could whip something up in a few weeks that would be commercial ... but it would have none of the enduring quality of *The Crackwalker*. I am not boasting when I say these things, because in writing both my plays, I have felt that I was nothing more than a hard-working vessel for the characters and images that emerged. I then apply the technique learned from years of immersion in the theatre and hope I get a play.

In order to write a good play, or to be a good vessel, one has to have an uncommon sensitivity to others, a quality that makes it impossible to survive in the workaday world. I'm not saying that people that work at so-called normal jobs aren't sensitive, but I think they have to steel themselves; they can't take every little knock personally; they can't afford to see the lies, the pain. Perhaps I overdramatize but then... Anyway, I respect the art of playwriting enough to think if it is possible, a writer should devote all her time to it.

So I think, if my dates are right, that I got that Marty Fellowship around then, and I started to write *White Biting Dog*, my second play, which took, altogether, about three years. Part of my research was auditing a course of Freud and doing intensive research on autism. I have never used those subjects directly, but the plays were infused with what I had learned.

That time was very magical, because we were just a couple, and I had all this time to do nothing but write a play (although I did oversee three other productions of *The Crackwalker*). We were poor, but when you are that poor you just need less. It never occurred to me to have more than one pair of shoes a season. In fact I wore my sandals until it was time for boots. I wore old clothes of my mother's, but felt very fashionable in them. A lot of my friends wore that kind of thing. I never even thought about getting my hair cut professionally; a friend did that, when I saw her. We were certainly never hungry, although we lived on about eleven thousand dollars that year, or maybe less. I had no obligations then, no web connecting me to King and Bay.

Now I have the most wonderful obligation in the world, a beautiful 21 month old girl, Ariane Francesca. I am working on about six or seven TV, radio and stage projects at once. I am asked to give readings and talks quite frequently. My beautiful obligation is just waking up from her nap. My first big screenplay, *Turning to Stone*, was due on my due date. But she was three weeks early, so in my first month as a mother I had to produce a two-hour screenplay. But a new baby is so easy in the daytime. She just slept in the Baby Matey or in her cradle while I did about two or three hours of work a day.

OUR SCHEDULE NOW: Ariane goes to a private daycare from nine until twelve thirty while I work at my new electronic typewriter. I pick her up and bring her home and give her some soup and toast. She usually falls sound asleep at her little table with a piece of toast and melted cheese in her hand. I wipe off her hands and face with a wet paper towel and carry her up to our bed. I put her down and take off her shoes. Her toes always do a sort of wiggle stretch when I do that. I put a blanket over her and she is gone for one to two hours. If I am tired I sleep with her; if I am busy, I work.

My husband comes home at about six or seven and I go out for a much-needed run, just to be out in the air, to get some exercise, to vent all the tension. We eat very late, nine or ten, often not particularly together, just catch as catch can, except Ariane, of course, is fed at about six, has her bath at about seven thirty, and is asleep by eight thirty. She is up by six thirty or seven, so we have about two hours to be together, read or even, horror of horrors, watch television. It is a wonderful thing when you've been reading or writing all day and you don't want to deal with the written word anymore! Just see a dumb story. Also, because I write for television quite a bit, I have to watch to remind myself of the differences between film and stage.

I am first and foremost a stage writer. That's where the poetry is. A screenwriter can do a little, but there are usually so many people in on the project, and so much money at stake, that the poetry is lost; it becomes about business or, if it is the CBC, pleasing the viewers (I think condescending to the viewers). I think I was lucky with my first big project, *Turning to Stone*, because John Kastner, the producer, kept all the editors away from me. He was my only advisor.

Still, there is nothing at all like the electricity on the stage, where you can create a moment of maximum visual and verbal poetry, where you can

Judith Thompson (Queen's 1976, National Theatre School 1979) receiving the Governor General's Award for Playwriting from Governor General Jeanne Sauvé, June 1985. CREDIT: Cana Press.

reach into the audience's unconscious and pull forth ancient primal emotions, kept hidden because they can be dangerous, but far more dangerous when they are hidden, and emerge in twisted unrecognizable forms.

There is such a sense of community, common humanity, in a strong theatrical experience, something that is sometimes found in a church, through ritual and worship, pausing for a couple of hours to really see ourselves, instead of rushing through daily life so fast that we are blinded. Because its aims are so high, they are rarely achieved in the theatre. When they are, I say to myself, oooooh yesss, this is what it's all about. This is ... something to do with eternity, with souls, without time.

Thanks for the help.

The warmth of Siberian hospitality

KATHERINE E. WYNNE-EDWARDS

Relatively few Canadians have the opportunity to spend time in Siberia. My three months there during 1984 were unarguably the most formative and influential months in my life. Scientifically, the research into the ecology and behaviour of the dwarf Siberian hamster was rewarding and worthwhile; personally, I faced many social and political issues which I had never confronted before.

When I enrolled at Queen's University in the fall of 1977, I listed my chosen major as Biology. That single title has encompassed a broad range of fields, each of which I have enjoyed as much or more than the last. As a second-year student I worked briefly on research with heat-shock mutations in *Drosophila* fruit flies. Flies carrying a single mutation in a specific gene were completely normal at 25°C, fell paralyzed from the air within seconds of exposure to temperatures of 29°C, and recovered equally quickly upon return to cooler temperatures. Genetics fascinated me and I was sure that my future lay in that field.

Then I applied for the St Andrews Exchange Fellowship. I didn't win; I went anyway. I was charmed by the town of St Andrews, Fife, and had visions of a year spent studying medieval history and literature. That was before I rode my bicycle down the hill to the Gatty Marine Laboratory and discovered that 1979-80 was the first time a degree in Marine Biology would be offered. Standing on the rocky shoreline of the North Sea it didn't take long to decide that this was the perfect time for me to learn about salt-water life. The class comprised only six students, and met nine until five, Monday through Friday. It was a marvellous year, with visiting lecturers from all over the UK, each convinced that his or her own topic was the most exciting. I learned about algae, fish, intertidal animals, the dynamics of oceanic currents, and used a scanning electron microscope to study the anatomy of the oyster eye. I also studied the embryonic development of a snail and debated the ethics of releasing research data

Katherine Wynne-Edwards dressed for the field in her Queen's Biology Department t-shirt, photographed outside the bog where the Siberian researchers managed to lose the bus in over its axles.

about the homing abilities of salmon. Biologists studying salmon that were carrying radio transmitters had discovered that large fish swam along the net lines and through the gaps where the nets were knotted to the poles. Releasing the information could increase the fisherman's haul dramatically, help the economy of the area, and possibly endanger the survival of the salmon population. I didn't entirely neglect the history of Scotland though. One of my roommates was a fountain of knowledge about walking tours, stone circles and sites of ancient treachery.

The Queen's biology department was extremely supportive of my work in St Andrews. I began a summer of research for my fourth-year thesis. This time it was fresh-water biology and I studied the fish population of a small, deep, chemically-stratified lake near Waterloo, Ontario. The stratification prevented the bottom waters from ever mixing with the surface waters and created a gradient in the water column that supported huge populations of some algae. As a result of the special physical properties of the lake, all of the fish had diets that differed from the diets typical of their species and foraging adaptations.

Now it was time to apply for graduate school. I gratefully accepted the advice of my professors and applied to Princeton University. I wasn't sure precisely what I wanted to study but I had decided that it was 'the behaviour and social organization of something small and furry'. I knew very little about mammals or their physiology and so came to Princeton to work with Professor Robert D. Lisk. Himself a graduate of Queen's, Dr Lisk studied the behaviour and neuroendocrinology of the Syrian hamster. He had heard of a species of dwarf Siberian hamster, just arrived in the United States via Romania and then Britain. Soon I had a thriving colony of over one hundred.

A small, photogenic animal, *Phodopus* was native to the steppes of Siberia, northern Mongolia and North China. Very little was known about the species in the wild but they were extremely social in my experience. Pairs remained together and older offspring helped to rear their younger siblings. I had found the general focus of my PhD. I began writing letters to the Soviet Union, China and Mongolia, hoping to make contacts which would allow me to come and study the hamsters in the wild.

Three years after I sent my first letters, I received one in return from Dr Alexei B. Surov of the Institute of Evolutionary Morphology and Animal Ecology (ISMEZ) in Moscow. Based on suggestions in the letters from Dr Surov and Academician V.E. Sokolov, I hastily purchased the radio transmitting and receiving equipment I would need to follow individual hamsters. The transmitters were smaller than a fingernail and ran on tiny hearing-aid batteries. The packages could be surgically implanted in the abdominal cavity of individual hamsters. I didn't do much more by way of shopping because the consensus at this end was that I would not receive a visa. Generally it is quite easy, as a senior scientist, to visit a research institution in Moscow or Leningrad. I was neither a senior scientist, nor did I plan to work at the Academy. I planned to live in the field with the hamsters and far beyond the administrative network established around foreigners in big cities. Even I had to agree that my prospects were not promising.

A scant six months after Dr Surov's initial letter, it was now less than 24 hours before my plane was scheduled to depart from New York and I was trying to place a phone call to Moscow, to Dr Surov, to ask why I had no formal recognition of a trip that began the next day. I spoke almost no Russian and had a very unsatisfactory conversation with a woman whose only asset was as slim a grasp of English as I had of Russian. Nevertheless, why be pessimistic? I sent a fellow graduate student to Washington, DC, that night. She arrived at the Soviet Consular Office at eight o'clock the next morning and joined a crowd of about 15 people in a small waiting room. Back in Princeton I began packing: batteries for everything in case there was no electricity; my radio antenna strapped to a tripod and protected with precious rolls of western toilet paper; strong Canadian insect repellent; twenty-five live-traps; a jar of peanut butter as bait; a soldering iron for the transmitters. Meanwhile, Lucy was calling from Washington every hour to tell me that no one in the consulate had ever heard of me and that I wasn't going anywhere. Her phone calls came at 10, 11, 12 and again at 12:45 to say that the office would close for the day at 1 pm. At 1:15 pm I got the last phone call. 'I've got your visa, I've got a taxi, I'm on my way to the airport.' Then, I packed in a genuine, excited panic. Eighty pounds overweight with my baggage, my plane took off from Kennedy airport the same evening at 7:20.

I had no real understanding what I was embarking on for three months in a place I knew almost nothing about. I only knew that the People's Revolution had occurred in 1917 because a friend had coached me. I knew the names of some of the tsars because they often showed up in crossword puzzles. In sum, I had an embarrassing lack of information. Over the past two months I had had one hour per week of tutoring in Russian. That meant that I could sound out the alphabet, identify the roof, floor, teacher and chalkboard, but only tentatively ask where the bathroom was.

Somewhere between Frankfurt and Moscow I pulled out the Berlitz guide I had bought in the airport and started trying to compose my first sentence. I need not have worried. After I cleared customs at Sheremetyevo, the next thing I saw was a sign bearing my name. I didn't understand a word but I was bundled into a car and taken to the Academy of Sciences Hotel. The next morning I boldly found my way to the buffet on the sixth floor. Ordering was tricky. I had to specify weight or volume for every purchase. I was on my second Fanta when Dr Surov appeared. For three days I was royally treated in Moscow while arrangements for our travel to Siberia were made.

We couldn't get tickets to the circus but we did get tickets to the opera. My second evening in Moscow was spent in a seat in the new Kremlin theater experiencing *Don Karlos* in Russian. During the days I walked, stared and met many of Dr Surov's colleagues. Some of them spoke excellent English and all were interested in hearing about my research and in telling me about their own. Their warmth and enthusiasm were infectious.

On the third evening I flew Aeroflot (the leg room is reminiscent of People Express) east. With me were Dr Surov, now called Alyosha, and one field assistant, Dimitri (Dima). We spent two days in Novosibirsk in the Academy Hotel in the Academ-Gorodok, the academic city. There I met my hosts from the Siberian branch of the Academy of Sciences, had a tour of a mink and sable research lab, and spent long hours in the museum laying preserved specimens of the hamsters out on maps so that I could determine exactly what their distribution was. By this point I was beginning to get a picture of the social environment I would be working in. It was somewhere between protectionist and chauvinistic. To photograph the maps I had to climb up to the rafters. I wasn't allowed to risk myself. None of the others could actually use my Nikon camera. I conceded, guessed the appropriate settings and have some poor photos. To this day I am not sure how many of the restrictions on my attempts to take minor risks were because I was a foreigner and how many were because I was a woman. Protectiveness was something I was not used to. It was hard for me to lead my life at the relatively relaxed pace at which the system operated. Their actions, however, certainly came from a genuine desire to make me happy and were not deliberately obstructionist.

Next we took the overnight train 500km southwest to Karasuk. There we were met by a genial bus driver named Sasha and driven to the Biological Station near the town of Troitskaya. I got my first look at home. We were on the border between a steppe (open grassland) and forest-steppe ecological zone. The land was extremely flat and the elevation was less than 250m above sea level. That was as close to a sea as I would come.

It was 2500 miles to the Indian Ocean, 2500 miles to the Arctic Ocean, 3100 miles to the Pacific and almost 4,000 miles to the Atlantic. On the globe, I was as far away from any ocean as it is possible to be. More immediately, I was to live with my field assistants in a tiny whitewashed house containing two bedrooms and a kitchen arranged around a central chimney. The outhouse was a quick 300 yard dash away and water was brought daily by tractor from the well in the village to a milk can outside the front door. The house had many amenities. I was given the big room, a desk, a set of shelves. We had an entry porch to leave equipment in and an attached bathroom area. The bathroom consisted of a sink through the slat floor to the ground and a water holder above to dispense water into the sink. I had remembered to bring a sink plug so everything was great. We had electricity, a fridge and a stove. The fridge held just my batteries, because our food was prepared for us in the dining hall by a wonderful babushka (an affectionate name for an old woman) who shared my name, Katia.

Other than the bootleg milk, our diet was atrocious and I was glad I had brought some good vitamins. We subsisted mainly on boiled last-year's potatoes. For breakfast and dinner we would have deep-fried fritters of cabbage. For lunch, the main meal, we ate bread, butter, broth made from fish stock, and extra helpings of boiled potatoes. In the entire stay I had only one meal which could not be eaten easily with a spoon. That meal was a goose, sacrificed from the research flock, that I prepared as a special meal for the camp. I'll never forget my naivete when I volunteered to prepare a goose, Canadian style. First, I was hauled down to the lake and asked to finger the individual I wanted. It took an adamant refusal before they realized that I did not want to kill it myself. Then, it was, of course, still fully feathered. Thanks to a poor graduate student, I had help with the plucking. He had never had a down pillow and offered to help if I would let him keep the down. The next step was a quick trip into the village to borrow a blow-torch to sear the last feathers. The rest was relatively easy and the result was a special treat for us all.

During my stay I cooked another meal which caused quite a stir. I had to plan two weeks in advance because I wanted cocoa (a two-week wait, and purchased in Novosibirsk) and black pepper (in a small jar off the mantel from the grandmother of one of the students). The black pepper went into a cream of mushroom soup for 45. Everyone collected mushrooms on sight. Even I was trained in good-mushroom, bad-mushroom within a day of their first appearance. The soup got mixed reviews. About half of the people had seconds. The rest poured theirs discreetly outside. The cocoa was the triumph. Mixing it with butter, I managed to make a thin layer of chocolate in the freezer and create passable chocolate chips. Chocolate chip cookies were a completely new experience for everyone in the camp. The only Soviet cookie that I ran across was a hard digestive biscuit. Over 200 cookies went down 45 throats in under two minutes.

Vodka was everywhere. Unfortunately it wasn't of Stolichnaya quality. In fact, it was indistinguishable from the ethanol I used to preserve specimens. Often when a villager helped us the payment of his choice was some of my preservative. I never drank any of it myself. I pulled my important foreigner strings and often received gifts of wine from anyone who had been to Novosibirsk. People were also generous with any fish they caught. I was always invited to a private (6-7 people) dinner whenever anyone had a special treat. I began to really appreciate the extent of the warmth and hospitality of the Soviet people.

Over the next three months I discovered many things about hamsters, and received two more field assistants from Moscow, Ilya and Sasha. Sasha was a relief in many ways. She was roughly my own age, a biology student at Moscow University; she spoke English, which no one else except Alyosha did, and she brought Ryetka with her. Ryetka is a fox terrier trained by Sasha's mother (a zoologist in the Moscow Academy of Sciences) to hunt for small mammals. We could toss her out in a field and she would search every burrow she could find. If it was occupied she began to dig. If the animal escaped out a back door, she knew instantly and we could give up. If we came to a fork in the tunnel, she always knew which direction to choose. Most of all she knew whether there were other animals after we had captured one so that we could have a complete census of which animals shared burrows. When we caught a hamster we would take it back to the station and I would surgically implant the small radio transmitter. We then released the animal in the same area the same day and could always locate it via the signal.

There were numerous social and technical difficulties and frustrations. I could not walk to the field area because I was a visiting scientist from America and therefore ought to be driven. I could not drive to the field area because there was no gas. When I pushed it seemed that we didn't know when there would be gas but 'spakoine.' That was one of my first idiomatic translations. It means 'take it easy' and, sure enough, I had to sit on my hands for two days when I would only have had a few miles to walk. Other days brought other delays. We lost the bus in a bog up over its axles and had to be rescued by a tractor that MacMillan-Bloedel would

A staged scene of Katherine and Alyosha taken by Dima the field assistant. 'After a complaint by me that they were doing all of the heavy work, Alyosha set out to have a picture of himself in a supervisory role while I dug a ditch.'

be proud to own. Then, we drove to the area where many of the correct species of hamster had been captured 4 years before and found it under 18" of water.

The best means of transportation was motorcycles. They are all painted camouflage green and look exactly like the German World War II issue, complete with side-cars. We also bought ourselves a little 50cc Riga motorcycle to help get me back and forth to the field. She was nicknamed Bison and I was very fond of her even though her kickstarter never worked and she needed a powerful shove to get going.

The mainstreet of the nearby village sported wall-to-wall ruts. Many of them were over a foot deep. It made the motorcycle side-car into a stomach churning experience. The ride was worth it though. I hadn't yet been allowed to prove that I could ride the motorcycle so the side-car was the only transportation. Every evening I would rinse out our milk jar and leave it with Anatoly. He would drive into the village and buy fresh milk – milked directly into our jar – for the amerikanskii. The village was a cooperative farm and was home to about 200 people. They weren't blessed with the most fertile soil but they grew grain and corn and kept a ranging herd of cattle. The single store contained very little, mostly cigarettes, rice and white sugar. Fresh bread came out every day from Karusuk.

Being the amerikanskii was an experience in itself. The people I worked with all knew that I was a Canadian although I currently lived in the United States. They had trouble believing that I could remain Canadian while taking my salary from an American institution and living in America. That certainly wasn't the only reason for the confusion though. For the vast majority of the Siberians, I would be the only foreigner from the west they could ever hope to meet. It was somehow more glamorous to have been pals with an American. Interestingly, when they occasionally verbalized dreams about visiting the west, I spontaneously became Canadian again. Canada wasn't necessarily attainable, but it was conceivable. A trip to America was impossible. By this point I hadn't mastered more than a tiny spoken vocabulary in Russian but I had a rapidly growing understood vocabulary. I could understand conversations and questions but I still had to pass anything but monosyllabic answers through Alyosha or Sasha.

There were lots of good things that came from my American luggage. Toothpaste did not need to taste like Comet cleanser. Insect repellent could work. Krazy Glue was incredible. The radio-telemetry techniques for following the animals were new. Swiss army knives were the strongest steel in camp, but the Walkman cassette recorder served the most varied

146

functions. It recorded data while I followed hamsters through the night. It sang to me in fluent English. It entertained the students and, certainly not least, it provided the first music that a deaf 13-year-old girl ever heard. Anatoly's daughter was almost completely deaf but she could feel the vibrations of the music when she adjusted the balance so that the bass was very strong. Needless to say, out of the long list of people who would have loved to own the Walkman, Anatoly was the one I left it with.

For a month the biological station was home to a group of 30 students on a field course from Novosibirsk University. They were intensely curious about me and about America. They even arranged a discotheque (with my cassette tapes) one evening. I think it was largely for the women to get the chance to watch me dance. I'm sure I didn't represent the most innovative North American dance styles, but apparently they were satisfied to learn that I didn't. That was intimidating but nothing compared to the next week. Four people were driving 18km overland to go swimming in a shallow saline lake. I agreed to go too and, suddenly, 25 people were coming. The sight of me in my bathing suit was not one to be missed. It was an ideal opportunity to assuage the nagging doubt that two peoples couldn't be so different politically without some underlying anatomical differences. For any that missed the lake, once every ten days we would fire up the sauna and each have a hot water splash-bath.

The greatest surprise came one evening near the end of the summer. A large party arrived from the zoo in Novosibirsk. They came to pick the currants that grow as windbreaks and to make 300 kilos of jam. The jam was for the animals, to provide them with a source of vitamin C during the winter. Needless to say, we were also busily picking and crushing currants for everyone to take back to Moscow. Everyone needed jam as a source of winter vitamins. The crowd cooked a huge meal in my honour and sang and danced all evening. I couldn't join them, though, for I was completely surrounded by a group of five women who were bombarding me with questions. These were not the usual shy questions. These women wanted to know the answers. Among the questions I answered over the next four hours: Are contraceptive pills like thalidomide? Instead of preventing pregnancy they had heard that the pills produced deformed children. Is there such a thing as an internal tampon? Is there a mandatory two-year military service in America? Didn't I carry a gun? That evening was a very moving experience for me. Not only did I begin to understand the extent of their ignorance about their own bodies, I found that all had had at least one abortion. Although abortion is illegal in the USSR, it seemed to be the only method of birth control.

Before I left Russia, I was taken on a quick weekend trip to Leningrad. It took many long hours of standing in line to get a visa but it was well worth it. The Hermitage and the Winter Palace were spectacular. I also dined on champagne and caviar for the last days in Moscow. It went a long way towards erasing my memories of the summer of potatoes. Unfortunately, I began to see that much of the best of Moscow was available to me as a privileged foreigner. The distinction between tourist and native was hard to deal with when we had all lived together so easily in Siberia.

When I returned to Princeton I brought back a changed view of the world and of the assumptions I had always taken for granted in our western world. I see the flamboyant coloration of packages trying to jump off the supermarket shelves into my cart, and I remember the village store that sold salt, sugar, rice and cigarettes. I see a Canadian cornfield before the harvest and remember that the cooperative farm I was on didn't get the corn above shoulder height by the end of August. Then I enter my apartment and see the wealth of little presents I was given as mementos and my heart fills up with warmth for the people who welcomed me and took care of me that summer.

It is now the summer of 1986 and I cannot begin to predict where I will be in the next few years. My PhD is almost complete. I am making tentative plans to go back to Russia next year, or perhaps to Mongolia where I can find wild hamsters belonging to the second species that I study in the laboratory. Soon, Canada will call me home, but that won't stop me from seeing an Amazon rainforest, an Australian kangaroo and who knows .....

Starting out

E. JANE WRIGHT

I am an entomologist, one who studies insects. Not a common profession for anyone but one that is attracting more and more women. I am 32 years old, unmarried and living on the other side of the world. I don't have a lifetime of sterling achievements to report, but I can relate some experiences and concerns of one of the younger generation of professional women.

I am the eldest of three children. Both parents and one grandmother are Queen's graduates. My father is a very successful businessman who seems to think I can do anything. My mother is a superb organizer and almost invariably ends up running any volunteer organization she joins. I grew up in an upper-middle-class home in suburbia outside Montreal and had the usual experiences growing up, Girl Guides, summer camp and braces on my teeth.

Most entomologists I know started out collecting butterflies or beetles as children. I didn't even know what a beetle was, technically, until I went to Queen's. Nevertheless, I was always interested in biology. In seventh grade, I was making infusions of dry grass and pond water and spending lunch hours looking down a microscope at ostracods. In high school I can remember being fascinated by the Golgi apparatus and frustrated because I discovered that very little was known about it at the time. I wasn't just interested in biology. Mathematics was a delight, especially geometry, and I was constantly winning hamburgers from the teacher for solving his so-called unsolvable problems. I enjoyed physics, especially being able to calculate the velocity of a ball at landing after it was thrown into the air off a cliff. A few concepts gave me some trouble initially, which led to my father's excellent advice that all I needed to remember was $f = ma$ and you can't push on a rope.

The formal learning part of high school was wonderful. The social part was a disaster. Because I liked to learn, I was ostracized, yet I desperately

Jane Wright examining African beetle samples, Brisbane, Australia, 1987

wanted to be popular. I resolved this problem partly by moving socially with students from a different school but I would never want to be a teenager again. My mother and I organized the high school graduation dance in my last year but I had to borrow my best friend's boyfriend from the other school for my date because no one from my school asked me. It didn't occur to me to do the inviting; things just weren't done that way. In any case my date was a success. We were good friends without the messy complications of hormones and my stock rose considerably as the others wondered where I had found this gorgeous man. It was a sweet victory from the jaws of defeat.

It was always assumed that I would attend university. Although my parents (Queen's Science '53 and Arts '58) staunchly maintained that they would never try to interfere with my choice of university, my grandmother (Queen's Arts '20) did not feel so restrained. In my last years of high school, lovely books about Queen's began to appear at home. On the way to the cottage in my junior college year, my father detoured through Kingston during engineering convocation weekend, 'just for fun.' The campus was beautiful, the weather was great and the men! I enrolled at Queen's the next year.

My first week at Queen's made a great impression. It was orientation week and, contrary to instructions, I had not learned the words to the Queen's songs in advance. After the first few hours of being forced to sing them again and again I knew the words well enough. On the first day I thought the whole exercise was absurd and childish. By the end of the week, I was convinced that Queen's was the best university in the world. Even after ten years I feel a special attachment to Queen's I don't have for the other schools I've attended.

I started out in mathematics but soon found that a subject being interesting just wasn't good enough anymore. Computers, however, were exciting and I could see that there would be infinite applications. I wanted to do a joint program with biology and computer science, but by the time the school had agreed to such a program I'd opted for straight biology. I was always planning my career around the last thing in which I'd an interesting course. First it was botany, then marine biology, then botany again and finally entomology. I took a simply wonderful entomology course from B.N. Smallman and A. West. The clincher came when I got a summer job working for R. Harmsen on a project at the Delhi Tobacco Research Station on parasites of the tobacco cutworm. The project was to be written as my undergraduate thesis and I went off armed with a piece of paper on which Harmsen had scribbled a few ideas. My supervisor

Jane Wright. Field work in Hluhluwe Game Reserve, South Africa, 1985

in Delhi had a copy of the same piece of paper, and so, with a minimum of guidance, I developed my own project. It was my first experience with research and practical entomology and I loved it. Entomology seemed the perfect profession. I could combine my interest in creepy crawlies and botany and do something that would really be useful. (Relevance was 'in' at the time.)

I also fared well socially at Queen's, where it was good to be smart. I 'majored' in engineers my first year, attending five formal dances with five different men. Sophomore blues allowed me time to bring the grades up again and during the last two years I made many good friends, male and female.

In my final year I quickly realized that a BSc in biology was not sufficient to get an interesting job. On advice from Queen's professors I went to Guelph to see about MSc studies. There were three faculty members in suitable areas. One of them growled at me the first time I met him in the coffee room and I was told by the other students that he didn't like female graduate students. Interviewing the other two took all day. A graduate student called me at home that evening to say that the ogre was disappointed I hadn't seen him so I summoned my courage and went back.

The early days as his student were rocky. John Laing seemed to feel that if he provided no encouragement or assistance and I quit (as had all his previous female students), then he wouldn't have wasted his time. My favourite fantasy was to finish my thesis, throw it on his desk, and quit. I recall one flaming row when we stood at opposite ends of the corridor and shouted at each other. He yelled that I didn't know everything and I roared back that that was why I was at school. We both grew up a little and I certainly learned to work independently. Now we are good friends and colleagues. I like to think that I am part of the reason that he now takes female students regularly.

Being a student in entomology at Guelph was all-consuming. We worked absurd hours, or at least we attended for those hours. How efficient was the work is a matter of opinion. Nevertheless, there was a great camaraderie and we were united in our love for insects. The department was terrific, probably the best I've seen, because people seemed to respect each other. Students felt they were members of the department and it was an excellent training-ground for entomologists.

Part way through my program there I realized that this, finally, was what I wanted to do for the rest of my life, to study insects and teach students. A faculty position requires a PhD. I applied to the University of California at Berkeley to study in the Division of Biological Control of the Department of Entomological Sciences and, to my surprise and delight, was accepted.

I left for California with some trepidation. I was completely awed by the reputation of the school and professors. And, it was in a different country. I soon discovered that I could cope academically. I thoroughly enjoyed the courses. The famous people turned out to be real people with warts and bumps like the rest of us, which helped considerably.

My major professor at Berkeley was Carl Huffaker, the renowned insect ecologist. He was almost at retirement when I arrived and hadn't taken any students for several years. He had been John Laing's professor and as a favour he took me on, with the understanding that I later would find someone else. When I had difficulty finding another supervisor he offered to see me through. It has been a great honour to be his last student. He was a perfect supervisor for me. He let me work on my own with a minimum of interference, yet was always there, ready to listen and give advice and support. Most PhD students in entomology at Berkeley give a seminar to the department at the end of their program. Because there is no formal defence of thesis, this tends to serve that purpose. It can be quite a harrowing experience. Just before mine, Carl arrived at the lecture hall with the first draft of my dissertation under his arm. He was preparing to give it back to me but I said that I could wait. While I was anxiously scanning the incoming crowd for the particularly difficult people, he came up again and told me I should at least read what he'd put on the top. It said, 'Congratulations. An excellent piece of work, well done and well written.' After that I could have slain dragons.

Degrees at Berkeley generally take longer than at schools in Canada, largely because of the heavy course load. My Natural Sciences and Engineering Research Council Scholarship lapsed before the end of my program. I applied for the Marty Memorial Scholarship to cover my last year of study; winning it enabled me to concentrate on writing up rather than trying to finish while holding a job.

Berkeley and California gave me the opportunity to broaden my horizons. I took up wildlife photography, white-water rafting and gourmet cooking. I discovered artichokes, enoki mushrooms, sushi and good wine. I gradually metamorphosed from the obsessed student to the more balanced professional.

Finding a job was quite a challenge. Unlike my office mate who applied for every position possible and papered her walls with rejection letters, I took a more selective approach. In the last eighteen months of my degree program only three positions came up that I felt were worth pursuing. I interviewed unsuccessfully (thank goodness!) for one, faced my first blatant case of sexual discrimination on the second, and landed the third, which was the one I'd considered a long shot. The post was with the Commonwealth Scientific and Industrial Research Organization of Australia to work at their overseas field station in South Africa. The project was to assess the suitability of the South African insect predators of dung-breeding flies for importation to control pest flies in Australia. I'd never had any interest in working overseas or even visiting Africa. I understood that Australians were male chauvinists and would never hire a woman for such a post. Still, jobs were mighty thin on the ground and I risked nothing by trying. (I later found that including myself there were four female research scientists in CSIRO Entomology and two of us were in South Africa. So much for preconceived ideas.) My parents were very pleased that I had finally finished school and got a job but my mother felt obliged to ask, 'But what shall I tell people you do?'

If leaving Canada for California was exciting, this was real adventure. After two frantic months in Australia I set off again to South Africa, to a country in social turmoil, a lab I'd never seen and colleagues I'd never met.

My first job had more than the average complement of ups and downs. The high point was doing field work in a game reserve full of rhinos, zebras, antelope and lions. We had a very nice lab built up on the hill and woke in the morning to the sound of monkeys scampering across the roof and zebra munching on the grass just outside the door. Hearing lions close by while waiting for a two-ton mother rhino and her calf to amble off the site made for exciting field work!

Making the transition from student to professional scientist was complex. As a student I had to do everything myself. As a scientist in charge of a lab group, I had to learn to direct others. People management was not taught in graduate school. I had to learn it the hard way, and within the unique social system of South Africa, to which I could never adjust. Shortly after I was promoted to officer-in-charge of the unit our funding was drastically cut. It fell to me to lay off fourteen locally engaged staff and close down a field station which had been in operation for seventeen years. Talk about trial by fire! I am now in Australia to write up my work until my contract expires in eight months.

The future is uncertain. My goal of a tenured faculty position may well be impossible. I am one of the new generation of short-term contract researchers. While this hiring form may be financially advantageous for institutions, it exacts a heavy price in research and personal lives. In the mad rush to publish ten papers from the current grant in order to get the next one, long-term work on knotty problems is an unaffordable luxury. We spend a fair proportion of our time on each contract trying to line up the next one. I chose entomology, aware of the limited employment opportunities. I felt that it was better to strive to be one of the very best scientists for whom there would always be employment, than to settle for second without a fight.

This pursuit of entomology as a career has meant moving away from family and friends at regular intervals. I have had several very special male friends but marrying would have meant compromising my career. I would like to marry one day when the situation and the fellow are right but am aware that, statistically, at my age my chances are slim. I take some comfort from an unmarried female scientist I greatly admire, who told me that she too had never married because of her career, but that she never regretted the decision. It is a sad commentary of our times that, in general, marriage assists men, but retards women, in their careers. I have decided to make my career my top priority and so far I'm happy about the decision. If, when I'm over eighty, I contribute to the Marty centennial volume, I'll let you know how it came out.

This life as painter

LEE KOZLIK

I

I am a fledgling Marty Scholar. I have no advantage of distance or perspective to write from. I am still very much living *in* my Marty Scholarship years, am still very much connected to the process I wrote about in my two applications to the committee. There is very little before and after, only a narrow space of time from which to sit back and say 'ah yes, those were the consequences, that was the result.'

I have only a Then and a Now – the Then, my Queen's life, first as a student for four years and then as instructor in the Department of Art for seven years, and the Now as full-time painter here in Europe, my painting life. The leap between Then and Now is due in great part to the support of the Marty Memorial Scholarship.

II

To tell you something about why I am trying to live a life here in Europe as a painter, I think I have to tell you something about circuses, somehow that explains a lot...

I know the word circus doesn't conjure up much for most Canadians if their memory is similar to mine: a rather faded half-hearted troup performing in a thawed out memorial hockey arena still stinking of hockey game, some lacklustre musicians who double as clowns and don't-even-try-to-hide-it, old toothless animals mangy in all the wrong spots – and not even as a child being able to squeeze out enough fantasy to shine up the lustreless atmosphere of nobody-quite-believing-anymore.

Shortly after I arrived here, people started talking about the Roncalli Circus coming. You can probably well imagine my confusion as I lined up with excited adults and over-excited children outside of a huge big top, lit like Eaton's Christmas windows, surrounded by painted and glittering Animal Crackers circus wagons, *real* clowns throwing buckets of confetti

Lee Kozlik before her painting, 'A Wasted Seduction', 1985, oil on canvas 130 × 200

as we entered, brass band music and sawdust and shinyness, and in November a warm summer afternoon tent smell. Here was a circus in all its glory, seducing you into its magic before it had even begun, full of its own spirit and aliveness. And then the performance, and the animals, and the scary acts, everything choreographed and sharp and shiny and as rich in its tradition and as intense as theatre or ballet. These circus people were professionals, and the audience too. Everyone recognized and participated in a tradition at once new in its richness and oldness. The Roncalli Circus came and went, overnight like all circuses must, but I knew I was in a different place. I had found a good place, and I must try to stay awhile.

III

To tell you about why I am a Painter, I have to tell you a little more about the circus ...

To be an artist in this world of Nobel Prize Winners is a dubious profession. It is especially questionable if one is a woman painter as it seems always to go back to 'oh that's an interesting hobby dear,' something to fill in the time nicely between the breakfast dishes, ironing his shirts, and having a good eye for colour, 'you have always been *so* creative dear.'

And if one manages to escape out of all that and works at her profession – going daily to an underheated studio at eight and coming home at five with only dirty fingernails to show and no idea of where the time went, one begins to question this profession where one uses litres of costly colour to cover kilometres of expensive canvas. What is the use of it? Where is the purpose? A brain surgeon, a Florence Nightingale, a lawyer, and a Jeanne d'Arc know what and why they are doing what they are doing. But the artiste who amazed us all by hanging from her hair and spinning at amazing speed at the very top of the big top of the Roncalli Circus probably never bothered with this question. And when she trained for hours, perhaps months, to grip a rope with her teeth and spin even faster in order to entertain us, I was convinced that spending my days with these colours was at least as fascinating as what she offered us. And when I lose my courage about this life as Painter, which I do almost daily, I find it again, almost always every day, if I think about the lady spinning at the top of the Roncalli.

IV

The leap from part-time academic/part-time painter to full-time Artist began with a resounding thump as I landed. My first application for scholarship support was not accepted so I began on my own with savings, optimism, a creative will and naiveté. What seemed so ideally easy – to spend each day in the studio working intensively – was terribly difficult. Gone was a built-in support system of colleagues and students, the security of a regular income and the corresponding pressure of lack of time. What remained was an empty studio, time and me. The dream which had become real life often bordered on nightmare as I learned how to work full-time with painting. I was solidly trained in the craft of painting (colour, shape, form), but for the realities of this new insecure existence, I was totally uneducated. I was at the beginning of, and am still living in, the process of learning to be an Artist, and all that it implies.

By the end of the first year I had managed to find some working solutions to these challenges. I had produced some work, exhibited, made new contacts, and began to realize what it meant to take oneself seriously professionally. My second application won me the Marty support and my education began in earnest. Because of the financial and psychological support this scholarship gives, being serious about being an Artist became easier. I say my education began in earnest because without this 'seriousness' from both sides (the giver and the receiver) education is only training.

So this leap has also somehow brought me full circle. During my studies at Queen's I received my training from men. Ten years after graduating I am (Now) receiving my education from women from Queen's.

V

To tell you something about why it has taken me this time to become a serious Woman Painter then I have to tell you about the Men ...

In all of my studies (at Queen's and at the University of Alberta), not one woman taught me Studio Art. Of course, in Art History (the genteel profession where one can be learned about art, simultaneously coiffured, manicured – one does not get dirty), there was one female Art History professor and a host of minor female positions. Ninety-eight percent of what we studied were works of art created by men. In the studio, where it counted, I was taught to paint, to print, to sculpt, and to think about the making of Art through the sensibilities and insensibilities of six men.

There was encouragement; there was praise; there was learning; there was excellent technical training. I know one, perhaps two, believed in (some of) us (the us in the beginning 20 females and 4 males). But *It* was there, the It of a group of women being taught by middle-aged men, the It of the subtle and not so subtle injustices, inflections, unstated words, and the overall lack of convincing evidence, either historical or

160

contemporary, to prove that what we were attempting to do could also be achieved by us, these young women.

In fact, there was also often an overwhelming contradiction or subversion in what these men were doing. Professor He said 'no woman can be a good artist' (not even great!); this same He taking the male students on a drawing field trip leaving 'the girls' behind, and sitting with the boys in the back of the room and rating 'us' by the size of our breasts, and then later, 'don't use that tone of voice with me girly.' And another happily married professor saying 'you can forget your work if you ever get married' and 'she's lost now that she has a baby,' and with these words stated so clearly and judgementally by these He's it takes very little fantasy to hear and feel the leftover and the unsaid.

Later, as half colleague of these Men – half because as Adjunct Academic one is in the no-man's-land of part-time contracts and tap dancing for renewals – I saw other women gradually come and go. They were always cheap (inexpensive) temporary replacements for these Men as they sabbaticaled through a year of artistic frenzy. I became friends with some of these men, I married another, but It was always there, perhaps It is still there. The same Men are there and there is still no woman on the full-time studio staff.

VI

And now you ask 'well, how did this all come about – this leaping and these Thens and Nows and Its and these Circus Stories?' I'm afraid the telling of this part can be as worn down as my mother's 78 rpm Glen Miller records, grooved and scratched always in the same places. The Then is best told from the immediate perspective from where it was seen.

A Short Personal History Written in 1984

I once watched a snake shed his skin. Discomfort alternating with relief, he stretched and contracted, and slowly, slowly pushed himself out the front end of himself. His skin lay behind him, transparent.[1]

Since graduating from Queen's almost ten years ago, I find myself here in Europe, living this life of Painter primarily through a process of 'stretching and contracting' alternating with 'discomfort and relief.'

During the last years at Queen's I also studied Art in England at the Falmouth School of Art and began my 'love affair' with British and European life and culture. I travelled for the first time to Paris in 1974

1 Anne Truit, Daybook, The Journal of an Artist, (N.Y., Pantheon Books, 1982) p.168.

and there came face to face with the major works of the 19th and 20th Century painters – all of which I had studied for so long in Art History classes through illuminated screens in darkened rooms. Once seen in real life, painting and its history took on new and dynamic dimensions. I could believe in it.

I was extremely fortunate to begin part-time teaching in the Department of Art at Queen's in 1975. I taught the Introductory Painting and Drawing courses and found the experience fulfilling and invigorating. By teaching two courses per year, teaching at the Agnes Etherington Art Centre to children and adults, writing for newspapers and journals, I was able to support myself, travel to Europe in summers, to paint in my 'free time,' and to exhibit.

I married another painter in 1977 and in 1978 we travelled to Greece for a year of painting in Crete. It was the first time I had the luxury of full-time painting. During this year I began to realize that only through full and concentrated activity can one produce a solid body of work.

On return to Canada with this work I was able to have two large one-man shows, one at the Agnes Etherington Art Centre, the other at a commercial gallery in Ottawa. This met with considerable success, 85% of the work sold and within one year the prices of my work increased 100%. This established me with several patrons and solidly launched my career.

I continued to teach at Queen's, as well as at other institutions, and was involved in many other art related activities and university related functions. I was increasingly involved with these activities and I found myself doing more talking about painting than painting itself.

As well, my private life made strong demands. I bought an old farm with my husband and built a studio. Attempting to live the role of wife, stepmother, teacher, writer, and painter became impossible.

This became an enormous conflict for me. In 1983 I travelled alone to France for three months to face this situation and attempt to either become more involved in my own work or to resolve this issue somehow.

I realized that I could not continue in this frenetic way (I too wasn't Superwoman). I decided I must do what was essential for me, and that, as I discovered in Greece, was to paint full time.

In 1983 I took a leave of absence from my job at Queen's and travelled alone to Europe. I found myself gradually healing and began to feel it possible to live as it is necessary for me to live in this European Culture as a Painter.

In March 1984 I made a difficult decision not to take my option to return to teaching at Queen's. I separated without financial support from my husband and soon will be divorced.

It has been an enormous step, and at times, extremely wrenching. Sometimes I feel myself floating in a lifeboat, set free and cast off from the mother ship. I sit in this little rocky boat and watch my supplies gradually dwindle, as my savings disappear. Other times it is a sensation of free falling without a net, at once exhilarating and frightening.

I know what I have chosen is right for me, although I often miss the cosy, full, comfortable Queen's life. It is difficult indeed, but a good difficult.

I wrote last year that once while lecturing I had the distinct impression of rubbing sandpaper across the flesh of my soul. I think now perhaps the soul is beginning to heal.

VII

To tell you how things are for me today, how depends very much on if it is a day where I have my courage or not. But the everyday realities do not change. I can report that I have as a studio a factory floor, an old coffee factory with a view of the churches and roofs of a town from the Middle Ages, that I paint and work there daily, that I am exhibiting, I am selling, I am learning lots the hard way, and perhaps what is most valuable to me, I am still struggling towards the ideals which I set forth in my first, indeed idealistic, application written in 1983:

I propose to paint with full force...I propose to meet an inner compulsion to discover the strengths and limits of my talents and abilities ...I propose to measure myself with the greatest of painting's history, and the newest of painters ... I make this proposal because I believe we have a moral obligation to test our talents. I have met the requirements and expectations others have for me, now I am trying to accomplish goals that are coming from within me ...

'Europe is rich in its traditions of aesthetics and culture. It embraces the artist in a manner which is unknown in North America. The artist is not an eccentric in the European Community ...

'I am asking for endorsement, encouragement, confidence and conviction on your part that it is possible to choose a path separate from the clearly marked road, that it is possible to live as an artist in our society. It would be an affirmation of a personal quest as well as the affirmation of place and role of the artist in society.'

List of Marty Recipients 1937-1987

1937   Winifred (Rutledge) Ireton
        Classics, University of London

1938   Jeanne S. (LeCaine) Agnew
        Mathematics, Radcliffe

1939   Honour to Elise M. Berry
        English, Queen's (Interrupted studies to serve in the Canadian
        Armed Forces)

1940   Anne H. (Sedgewick) Carver
        History, Radcliffe

1941   Eleanor (Clarke) Hay
        Endocrinology, McGill

1942   Joyce Hemlow
        English, Radcliffe

1943   Kathleen (Butcher) Whitehead
        Mathematics, University of Michigan

1944   Ellen Thibaudeau
        English, Radcliffe

1945   Reta (Anderson) Wood
        Bacteriology, Cambridge

1946   E. Claire (Curtis) Tanner
        Botany, Iowa State

1947   Barbara Rooke
        English, University of London

1948 Honour to Audrey D. (Freeman) Campbell
      French, University of Paris

      H. Arliss Denyes
      Biology, University of Michigan

1949 Pauline Jewett
      Political Studies, London School of Economics and Oxford

1950 Marion Robins
      French, University of Paris

1951 Sister Thelma-Anne McLeod
      English, Radcliffe

1952 Honour to Doreen E. (Maxwell) Hotchkiss
      Biology, McGill

1953 Llewellya (Hillis) Hillis-Colinvaux
      Botany, University of Michigan

1954 Honour to Ausma Rabe
      Psychology, University of Michigan

      Joan (Watson) Campbell
      French and Spanish, University of Toulouse

1955 Ausma Rabe
      Psychology, University of Michigan

1956 Honour to Elizabeth Catherine (O'Neill) Dempster
      Classics, American School of Classical Studies, Athens

      Margaret E. (Cornett) Green
      Botany, Radcliffe

1957 Germaine L'Abbé
      French, University of Paris

1958 Mary O. Conlon
      Economics, Columbia

1959 Barbara J. (Excell) Hawgood
      Physiology, Oxford

1960 Asta Helena Lepinis
      German, Queen's

1961	Marjorie (Smith) Allen Chemistry, University of Manchester
1962	Mabel I. Corlett Mineralogy, University of Chicago
1963	Honour to Janet P. Bews Classics, University of London
	Esther (Jamieson) Magathan Geology, Reading
1964	Janet P. Bews Classics, University of London
1965	Honour to Patricia G. (Reid) Dirks History, University of Toronto
	Honour to Virginia Killby Medicine, McMaster
1966	Joyce E. (McKee) Frakes German, Stanford
1967	Jane M. (Matthews) Glenn Law, University of Strasbourg
1968	Judith E. Martin Psychology, University of Illinois
1969	H. Dawn (Melvin) Aspinall English, University of Toronto
1970	Elspeth H. (Wallace) Baugh Psychology, York
1971	Elspeth H. (Wallace) Baugh Psychology, York
1972	Elfreda H. Epp Theatre Arts, University of London
1973	Patricia L. (Barr) Zelonka Mathematics, Queen's
1974	Elizabeth M. (Roach) Michalska Psychology, Queen's

Honour to Margaret Lynne (Thurling) Quinn
English, McMaster

1975   Michal (Ben Gera) Ben Gera-Logan
Political Studies, Yale

Leslie O'Dell
Theatre Art, University of Toronto

1976   Priscilla A. (Peebles) Galloway
Education, University of Toronto

Colleen Anne Purdon (special award)
Music Therapy, Guildhall School of Music and Drama

1977   Judith E. Mack
Psychology, York

1978   Linda Marie (Round) Buckland
History, Carleton

1979   Allessandra M.V. (Cavaglia) Duncan
Mutagenesis, University of Edinburgh

Mary Catherine Collins
Art Conservation, Indianapolis Museum of the Arts

1980   Susan Ray Craig
Biology, Queen's

Ruth Ellen (Allen) Lippett
Education, Queen's

1981   Cathy Stewart
Art Conservation, National Gallery of Canada

Anne Monaco
Music, Private Study in Chicago

Judith Thompson
Drama, Writing the play, *White Biting Dog*

1982   E. Jane Wright
Entomology, University of California (Berkeley)

Anna (Kerson) Smol
English, Queen's

Kathryn McConnell
Music, Johns Hopkins

1983 Allison M. Gagnon
Music, Vienna Academy of Music

Judith Thompson
Drama, Playwriting

1984 Katherine Wynne-Edwards
Biology, Princeton

1985 Lee Ann Kozlik
Art, Painting in Europe

1986 Donna Jeanne Vittorio
English, Queen's

1987 Catherine Higgs
History, Yale